THE ART OF BUILDING A
GARDEN CITY
Designing new communities for the 21st Century

RIBA ⋕ **Publishing**

© The Town and Country Planning Association, 2017

Published by RIBA Publishing, part of RIBA Enterprises Ltd, The Old Post Office, St Nicholas Street, Newcastle upon Tyne, NE1 1RH

ISBN 978-1-85946-620-9

British Library Cataloguing-in-Publication Data
A catalogue record for this book is available from the British Library.

Commissioning Editor: Fay Gibbons
Production: Richard Blackburn
Designed & Typeset by Kalina Norton
Printed and bound by Page Bros, Norwich, UK
Cover image credits: Nadia Taylor - agencyrush.com

While every effort has been made to check the accuracy and quality of the information given in this publication, neither the Author nor the Publisher accept any responsibility for the subsequent use of this information, for any errors or omissions that it may contain, or for any misunderstandings arising from it.

www.ribaenterprises.com

THE ART OF BUILDING A
GARDEN CITY

Designing new communities for the 21st Century

Kate Henderson, Katy Lock, Hugh Ellis

CONTENTS

CONTENTS

PART 2
DELIVERING THE FUTURE

Rt Hon Nick Raynsford

*President of the Town and
Country Planning Association*

We all know that Britain is facing an acute housing crisis. We are not building enough new homes, and too many of those that are being built are simply not affordable to those in need. But simply increasing the output and improving the affordability of new homes is not enough. We have in the past, too often, allowed quality to be subordinated to quantity and we have not always given sufficient attention to place-making – creating communities where people can thrive and feel good about their surroundings. Successful places also have to respond to a number of additional challenges, including providing for the needs of an ageing population, accommodating the inevitable advances in technology, and adapting to the consequences – as well as helping to minimise the threat of – climate change.

In this context, the legacy of the Garden City movement has a real relevance today. It was born from a determination to transform the living conditions of millions of people trapped in squalid and unhealthy slum housing in the industrial cities, and inspired both by an idealistic aspiration to create a better society and a deeply practical understanding of how to make things happen. The Garden City movement played a pivotal role in improving housing standards in 20th century Britain and also inspired the objective to create better communities that would combine the best of both urban and rural environments. The principles that underpinned the Garden City movement are more than ever relevant in today's society.

The Art of Building a Garden City sets out those principles and demonstrates how they can be applied in the 21st Century context, to deliver effective, credible and lasting solutions to the very real problems we now face. This is not just about good planning and design, which are of course essential to creating special places. It is equally about financial models which allow the proceeds of the development process and prudent stewardship of the assets to be applied in ways that sustain the vitality of the community in future years. This is a book about possibilities. It aims to reignite the ambition and enthusiasm for placemaking that this nation once pioneered. Above all, it is a reminder of what can be achieved when we put human needs at the heart of the housing debate.

SPONSORS

Lady Margaret Patterson Osborn Trust

The Lady Margaret Patterson Osborn Trust was set up by the children of Sir Frederic Osborn and his wife in memory of their mother. The Trust's remit is to promote interest in garden cities, new towns and other new settlements, and in Welwyn Garden City.

Bournville Village Trust

Bournville Village Trust was founded by George Cadbury in 1900 to help deliver a mixed community for people from a wide range of backgrounds, not only for the workers at the chocolate factory. The Trust is one of the longest-established housing associations in the country, with a successful history of creating and sustaining flourishing communities.
www.bvt.org.uk

Garden City Developments CIC

Garden City Developments is an independent community interest company. The CIC works with partners to apply Garden City Principles to create sustainable new communities.
www.gardencitydevelopments.org

Joseph Rowntree Housing Trust

The Joseph Rowntree Housing Trust was established in 1968 to take over responsibility for the housing operations of the Joseph Rowntree Memorial Trust (now known as the Joseph Rowntree Foundation - JRF). Today the Trust is a charity and registered social landlord providing housing, care homes, retirement and supported housing, and demonstrates new approaches in these areas.
http://www.jrht.org.uk/

Letchworth Garden City Heritage Foundation

Letchworth Garden City Heritage Foundation is the successor to First Garden City Limited, which from 1903 developed the world's First Garden City in Letchworth. The Heritage Foundation is a community benefit society, working for the benefit of Letchworth Garden City communities. This is primarily by way of reinvesting a surplus from its mainly property-based portfolio, which generates an endowment income, into the delivery of direct charitable services and charitable grants for local groups and individuals.
www.letchworth.com

WEI YANG·ı·PARTNERS
DELIVERING INTEGRATED MASTER PLANS

Wei Yang & Partners

Wei Yang & Partners has an international portfolio of town and country planning, master planning, urban design and architectural projects. The company is a member of Westminster Sustainable Business Forum, a high-level coalition of key UK businesses, parliamentarians, civil servants and other organisations, seeking to promote effective sustainability policy in the UK.

The firm has developed strong expertise in Garden City planning. The company's submission on New Garden City in Britain won the Finalist Award of the Wolfson Economics Prize 2014 from 279 entries worldwide.
www.weiyangandpartners.co.uk

ACKNOWLEDGEMENTS

The Art of Building a Garden City is the authors' overview of the Town and Country Planning Association (TCPA)'s campaign for a new generation of garden cities. This is the latest expression of over a century of the TCPA's thinking, learning and exploration of practical solutions to creating an environmentally resilient and socially just society. We are indebted to the garden city pioneers and former TCPA teams who continue to provide us with a mixture of inspiration and a sense of responsibility!

We would like to thank all of our colleagues and the Trustees, Policy Council and Vice Presidents of the TCPA for their enthusiasm for planning and belief in the utopian tradition.

We would particularly like to thank those who helped us bring this book alive with images, including our colleagues Nick Matthews, Hilde Steinacker, Alex House, Casey Parsons and Katrin Witte at the TCPA. We would also like to thank Josh Tidy and Vicky Axell at Letchworth Garden City Heritage Foundation, Claire Morrall at Bournville Village Trust, Paul Capewell at Hampstead Village Trust, Claire Vinent and Joanne Lofthouse at Joseph Rowntree Housing Trust, David Lock, Nadia Taylor, David Barnes, Pam Warhurst and Estelle Brown at Incredible Edible, David Bostock at the Radburn Association, Gilly House, Leila Fielding, Will Cousins and Caroline Brown from David Lock Associates, Tony Skottowe and Vanessa Godfrey at Welwyn Garden City Heritage Trust, Kate MacTiernan at Shuffle Festival and Dawn Kayse and Alison Cahn at Lancaster Co-Housing, Hannah Emery-Wright at ELCLT, David York and Anne Thorne at Cannock Mill Co-housing, and all other contributors for their assistance with images.

The book would also not have been possible without the generous support of our sponsors.

Many thanks to the team at RIBA Publishing, in particular to Fay Gibbons for approaching us about this opportunity and supporting us throughout the process along with Richard Blackburn and Elizabeth Webster.

Finally, we would like to thank our families and friends for their patience, love and support.

ABOUT THE AUTHORS

Founded by Sir Ebenezer Howard in 1899 to promote the idea of the garden city, the Town and Country Planning Association (TCPA) has been at the forefront of delivering new communities for over a century. The TCPA is an independent charity campaigning for the reform of the UK's planning system, to make it more responsive to people's needs and aspirations and to promote sustainable development. The association occupies a unique position, overlapping with those involved in the development industry, the environmental movement and those concerned with social justice, and prides itself on leading-edge, radical thinking and problem-solving.

Together, the authors of this book have been leading the TCPA's campaign for a new generation of beautiful, resilient and inclusive garden cities for the 21st century.

Kate Henderson

Kate Henderson is chief executive of the TCPA, where she leads the association's efforts to shape and advocate planning policies that put social justice and the environment at the heart of the debate. Kate has raised the TCPA's profile through a range of high-profile campaigns, research projects and policy initiatives, most notably around garden cities, affordable housing, poverty and climate change.

She has been involved in a number of government panels and independent commissions, including the independent Lyons Housing Review.

Kate is a visiting professor at the Bartlett School of Planning at University College London and a member of the Board of the International Federation of Housing and Planning. She regularly appears in the national and trade press and she has co-authored two previous books with her colleague Hugh Ellis.

Katy Lock

Katy Lock is the TCPA's garden cities and new towns Projects and Policy Manager and leads on the association's campaigns and promotion of garden city principles in policy, education and the arts.

Katy is a chartered town planner and has a MRTPI and a background in planning, urban design and sustainability. Before joining the TCPA in 2011, she worked for several years in the private sector as an environmental planning consultant. Katy is currently a trustee for Planning Aid London.

At the TCPA, Katy manages the organisation's policy strand *Creating garden cities and suburbs today,* including facilitating and reporting on cross-sector workshops and seminars, project managing and creating guidance and campaign documents and promoting the garden city model through seminars, events and lectures and in the media. She has worked closely with international organisations concerned with the garden city movement, including the International Federation for Housing and Planning

Katy is currently working on a practical guide to meeting the high standards of garden cities, a research project looking at transferable lessons from the new towns, and exploring how best to update the New Towns Act to deliver a new generation of garden cities

Dr Hugh Ellis

Dr Hugh Ellis is Director of Policy at the TCPA, where he leads innovative research projects and campaigns and provides expert planning advice and policy analysis.

From 2000 to 2009 Hugh was National Planning Advisor to Friends of the Earth England, Wales and Northern Ireland. He holds a Diploma in Town Planning, a Bachelor of Arts (with Honours) in Urban Studies and a Doctorate in Land Use Planning from the University of Sheffield. After spending a number of years working for the Coalfield Planning Cooperative on community planning projects Hugh took up a teaching and research post at the University of Sheffield, where his key interests were sustainable development and community participation.

Hugh has published two books on the future of planning and place making with his colleague Kate Henderson and is currently leading work streams around climate change, social justice and the Raynsford Review of the English planning system. Hugh is a honorary professor in the School of Planning, Architecture and Civil Engineering at Queens University Belfast.

The idea of the garden city is one of the most radical, practical and relevant legacies of the British town planning and utopian tradition. The garden city pioneers aspired to provide a blend of environmental sustainability, social inclusion and steely economics; they set out a pathway to a new kind of mutualised community with the highest standards of design accessible to all, and with the profits of rising land values shared for the benefit of everyone. The garden city was an idea of global significance, sparking an international movement and dialogue about progressive place-making.

In the context of the early-21st-century housing crisis, the garden city model has become politically fashionable, even if its core principles are often misunderstood. For some, it is shorthand for low-density housing with gardens for 'nice' people with a labrador and three cars. For others, it conjures up some kind of suburban hell. The confusion is not new; even within 20 years of the founding of our first garden city at Letchworth in 1903, the idea had been used to justify all kinds of housing development that had little or nothing to do with the high aspirations of the garden city movement. It is easier to trade these parodies than to examine the real lessons of the delivery of garden cities – something that this book aims to address.

In the same way, the postwar new towns programme, inspired by the garden city movement, is often derided and dismissed as a simplistic failure. There were, of course, mistakes, but the programme was in fact a remarkable success in meeting housing needs at speed. Its legacy looks even more significant in an era when Britain has largely failed to build any ambitious new communities; despite having world-leading design and masterplanning skills in the UK, we seem determined to ignore our own increasingly desperate domestic need to deliver inclusive and high-quality places.

The Garden City Ideals

The garden city vision was distilled by Ebenezer Howard from a rich tapestry of utopian ideas that swirled around the art and culture of the late Victorian period. It combined John Ruskin's romantic concern with the transformational impact of art and nature on human wellbeing, with socialist and anarchist ideas about the fair distribution of land and practical solutions to transport and sanitation. This was set within a context not of rejecting existing cities, but of a specific reaction to unregulated capitalist growth of urban areas and the abject poverty and inequality that marked, and continues to mark, their streets. The design of garden cities as envisaged by Howard provided a web of solutions to how we could live, from energy and local food to access to green space and health care, and provided new forms of education and business. What is truly impressive is that Howard found a way, not without difficulty, of funding such places

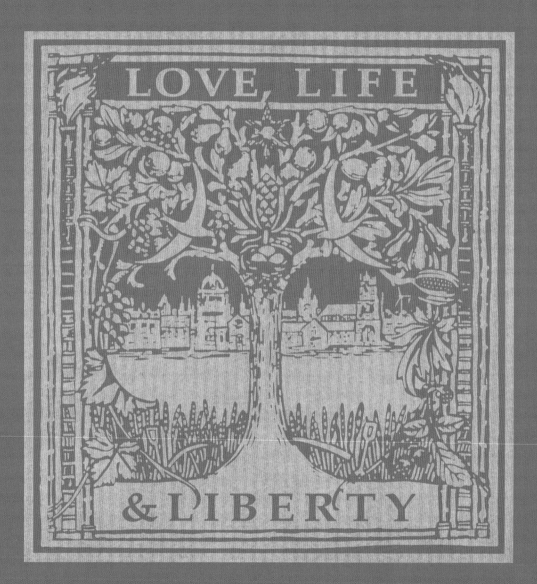

Cover of TCPA album 'Love, Life and Liberty' produced in 2012

based on a very simple model, which is at the heart of the garden city approach: part of the substantial increase in values that arise from the development of land should always be reinvested into the community for the benefit of all. Such a principle still sustains a whole range of services in Letchworth that other communities can no longer afford as a result of enforced austerity.

The reason garden cities and new towns have again become part of mainstream political debate is precisely because of the scale of the housing crisis facing the nation. This crisis is complex, and goes beyond the shortage of homes we are building to acute affordability problems and homelessness driven by a failure to build social housing in any meaningful quantity. The crisis is also about the often poor design quality of the new homes being built today, and whether communities have adequate services and infrastructure. A former planning minister described much new housing as 'pig ugly', and his assessment was plainly accurate. We are also slipping behind other nations who see the deployment of new technology in the built environment as a normal part of building the future. At a time when Germany can produce *Passivhaus*, our own government has abandoned not just any place-making policy but key standards such as Zero Carbon Homes.[1]

In this bleak and insular context, particularly in the aftermath of the 'Brexit", the garden city concept offers one thing above all else: hope of a better future, recapturing the creativity and enthusiasm of communities to build a lasting legacy of inclusive and high-quality places that meet the challenges of tomorrow. It offers an alternative to the sterile economics of austerity by showing how the fair distribution of land values can help fund resilient communities over the very long term.

This book aims to provide an overview of the development and delivery of garden cities and new towns, suggesting how that experience could form the basis of a new generation of highly sustainable and socially just communities.

Part 1 provides an overview of how the garden city emerged from the rich British utopian tradition, which blended art, economics, psychology and design into a powerful case for change. Chapters 1 to 4 document this history, from the English Civil War to the now much-derided eco-towns programme, framed by honesty about what worked and what did not. Chapters 5 and 6 go on to set out the challenges facing the nation today, and make the case for why new garden cities are part of the solution to these issues in the 21st century. Having assessed what we can learn from the past, Part 2 then sets out some of the kinds of approaches and standards that might shape new garden cities today. It examines some of the best UK and international examples of how change can be delivered.

The intention of this book is to explore the principles and values that should inform the design and delivery approach for new garden cities; it does not aim to specify a specific design approach or style. Above all, it is designed to help reignite the ambition and enthusiasm for place-making that this nation once pioneered, and aims to provide a message of hope with a vital relevance for the future of our society. ◆

LIVE IN THE SUN
AT
WELWYN
GARDEN CITY

PARTICULARS OF HOUSES AND SITES FROM ESTATE OFFICE, WELWYN
GARDEN CITY, HERTS. & KNIGHT FRANK & RUTLEY 11 HANOVER SQ. W. 1

*The garden cities offered a new way of living, far from the
inner-city slums of the late 19th and early 20th centuries.*

PART 1

◆ *One of the striking features of the debate about British planning and place-making has been the headlong decline in the quality and ambition of the arguments over the last 40 years. Many of the key successes of the garden city movement – and particularly its British successor, the new towns programme – have now been mythologised into failures. In an attempt to undo this confusion, Part 1 looks at the history and development of these communities, demonstrating that the past is in fact a repository of rich and radical learning that is still refreshingly creative and relevant today.*

chapter 1

A SHORT HISTORY OF
THE UTOPIAN TRADITION

This chapter takes us on a journey through the history and radical origins of the garden city movement, starting in the 16th century and exploring the influence that notions of ideal communities have had on the debate about future of design and place-making. It provides an overview of the debate about land and freedom during the English Civil War in the 17th century – which sparked new movements and ideas from groups like the Levellers and the Diggers – through to rich debates about the future of society at the end of the 19th century, and the first attempts at building new communities based on utopian thinking. It was out of this rich cultural mix of politics, art, economics and high moral ambition that the garden city movement emerged.

The 16th Century:
Thomas More's *Utopia*

Thomas More's *Utopia* was written in 1516, and marks the start, in Britain, of the concept of utopia as a powerful and often subversive political idea.[1] More's book describes an ideal community in which the laws and social organisation support what, for the time, was a highly egalitarian society. What makes *Utopia* stand out from the surprising number of contemporary 16th-century polemics attacking the ruling class is the level of positive detail about how this new community would develop.

The book, which was originally titled *The Best Condition of a Society*, was part of the emerging European humanist philosophy, but its focus on the ideal city state made it a key milestone in what later became known as the 'utopian tradition'. This movement was defined by calls for land reform, equality and democracy, but uniquely sought to cast these and other ideas in the context of the design of ideal places rather than abstract political ideas. Utopian thinking used to be part of mainstream politics, and was deeply embedded in our culture. It evolved over time to address everything from land reform to beauty in design, to new forms of economics. It was a rich tradition that formed the intellectual and political foundation from which the garden city ideals emerged.

However, despite this long-term legacy, *Utopia* had little practical political impact on 16th-century society. It took the devastation of the English Civil War in the 1640s to revive interest in More's vision and to prompt a resurgence in radical ideas of planned utopian communities from groups like the Levellers and the Diggers.

"England is not a free people, till the poor that have no land, have a free allowance to dig and labour the commons..."

Gerrard Winstanley, 1649

Fig 1.01
The Diggers were forced to leave St George's Hill in August 1649 following attacks and challenges in the courts.

The 17th Century: Land and Freedom

The great Putney Debates, which took place in 1647 between the officers and soldiers of Oliver Cromwell's New Model Army, examined how a new constitution could be founded on democracy, civil rights and land reform. It was a very modern political debate about the ideals of utopian society founded on a strong sense of civil rights and social justice. But in the aftermath of Cromwell's final victory over King Charles I in 1649, the new commonwealth was seen by many as betraying the promise of a new society. The Diggers were one group that tried in several places to found new communities based on equity and land rights (Fig 1.01).[2] They occupied common land and started to farm, believing that no one had any right to own land for their own personal profit. Their great advocate, Gerrard Winstanley,[3] wrote the most powerful call for land rights for the poor ever written in the English language in his *Declaration from the poor oppressed People of England*. The opening of the declaration still has a very modern resonance:

We whose names are subscribed, do in the name of all the poor oppressed people in England, declare unto you, that call your selves lords of Manors, and Lords of the Land, that the earth was not made purposely for you, to be Lords of it, and we to be your Slaves, Servants, and Beggers; but it was made to be a common Livelihood to all.

Like many who have come after them, the Diggers underestimated the risk they took by challenging the nature of land ownership. Their community at St George's Hill in Surrey suffered violent attacks from the local landlord, and proved to be a short-lived experiment. The story of St George's Hill has almost comic irony, in that the site is now partly a golf course and partly a gated community for the super-rich (Fig 1.02).

The 18th and Early 19th Century: The New Industrial Age

Utopian ideals remained a mainstream part of political debate throughout the 18th and 19th centuries. This period saw two powerful forces of social change – the enclosure of common land and industrialisation – both of which eventually led to perhaps the greatest creative period of change based on utopian thinking.

Enclosure of the Commons

Common land provided poor rural workers with the right to graze animals and collect firewood. From the time of Thomas More, landowners had sought to enclose common land, removing these rights and, in the process, creating desperate economic hardship. Each common enclosure required a new act of parliament, but since parliament was dominated by landowning interests the outcome was never in doubt. In Scotland and Ireland, people were dispossessed not just of their livelihoods but also their homes through forced evictions by private landlords. Overall, the enclosures amounted to the greatest transfer of collective ownership to private landlords in our history, and drove rural workers into the growing industrial cities in unprecedented numbers. These people had no land rights, and, as a result, no political rights.

The dramatic impact of enclosure on the welfare of the rural poor resulted in calls for land reform and even for the nationalisation of land, which became a mainstream part of political debate. Gerrard Winstanley's question of why a minority should own and profit from the primary resources of the Earth was taken forward by those such as the American writer Henry George.[4] In his 1879 book *Progress and Poverty*,[5] George argued for the common ownership of land and, crucially, for a single land tax that would allow the wealth of land ownership to be fairly distributed.[6]

Fig 1.02
A private tennis club
on St George's Hill today.

9

Close N.º 118 High Street.
1868.

Industrialisation

If land enclosures were one driver for land reform amongst utopian thinkers, then rapid industrialisation was the other. By 1850, more than 50% of the British population was housed in the country's expanding industrial cities. It is not fair to characterise these cities as places of universal poverty. In fact, they are better defined by their inequality between social classes and the physical separation of working people from the growing middle class. However, life for working people was both hard and short. Without regulation, urban development was characterised by cramped and unsanitary housing – and, as a result, disease was rife (Fig 1.03). Friedrich Engels in his 1845 work, *The Condition of the Working Class in England*,[7] provided an influential testament to the result of unregulated markets, and inspired subsequent studies into the industrial poor by Victorian social reformers such as Charles Booth and Beatrice Webb.

Fig 1.03
Glasgow slum developments in 1868: The garden city idea was part of a wider movement to address poverty and social inequality in Britain's industrial cities.

Fig 1.04
Chartists' house in Charterville, Oxfordshire, now in private ownership.

The flowering of new communities

Reform proved to be slow, mainly because the working-class poor had no vote and so no political power. Protest movements did exist, and Chartism[8] succeeded in bringing about a slow increase in the electoral franchise. What is now largely forgotten is that this movement also set up its own communities, including Charterville in Oxfordshire (Fig 1.04). The idea was that people would pay a subscription to buy tracts of land and would then receive a smallhold farm. The project was heavily oversubscribed but the financial model was flawed, with many finding it impossible to make a living out of their land allocations.

Experiments in new ways of living thrived in the 19th century – perhaps most famously at places such as New Lanark, Saltaire, Port Sunlight, New Eastwick and Bournville, where industrialists, inspired

Fig 1.05
New Lanark, providing homes and facilities for workers alongside cotton mills, was founded in 1786 by a partnership that included the social reformer Robert Owen. Today New Lanark is recognised as a UNESCO World Heritage Site.

by nonconformist religious belief, saw a moral and economic case for creating good conditions for their workforce. While influential in showing what might be achieved in relation to design, masterplanning and social provision (Figs 1.05–07), these places were remarkable exceptions to the general rule. For the majority, reform came slowly – driven by fear of unrest and disease, and by the growing labour movement. It found expression in basic rules for housing and sanitation ('By-Law housing'), which shaped tens of thousands of red-brick terraced homes that still characterise much of post-industrial Britain. The need for decent living conditions was a practical driver for change, and the end of the 19th century saw the coming together of practical needs and the ideals of the utopian tradition – not least, for the fairer distribution of land values.

The Late 19th Century: The Arts and Crafts Movement

The most influential expression of the utopian tradition was the emergence of the Arts and Crafts movement. John Ruskin was an important figure at the start of this movement, and his great contribution to the utopian cause was the ambition to hold together in one idea what would now be regarded as incompatible principles. He believed in the vital importance of preserving the natural environment while simultaneously campaigning for new and better housing for working people. For him, fulfilling lives were based not just on productive work but on access to the best art and architecture. Development that was well designed was a *complement* to nature, not its destroyer.

Fig 1.06a / 1.06b
Port Sunlight was built by
Lever Brothers from 1888 to
accommodate workers in its
soap factory.

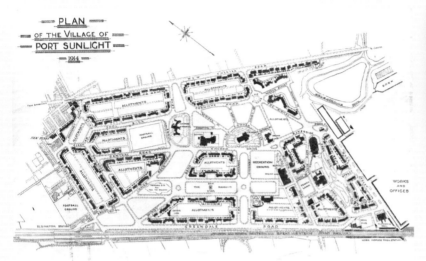

Fig 1.07a / Fig 1.07b
In 1893 George Cadbury
bought land at Bournville to
develop a model village for
factory workers – an early
'Garden Village'

Ruskin was a direct inspiration on the work of William Morris, who has claim to be the key figure in the flowering of the Arts and Crafts movement. Morris's work deserves to be read because it goes to the heart of many modern debates about the nature of work and the dehumanising effect it can have on people and society. His books *A Dream of John Ball*[9] and *News from Nowhere*[10] had a direct influence on the founders of the modern welfare state – not least Britain's first postwar Labour prime minister Clement Attlee, who recognised Morris as a key inspiration for the 1945 Labour Government.

Morris was a vital link in a chain of inspiration embodied by the 1880s in a group of contemporaries who did more than any other to shape garden city ideals. The group met around the table of Edward Carpenter, the socialist writer who campaigned for equality, land reform, vegetarianism and gay rights (extremely brave, some 80 years before homosexuality was decriminalised). Carpenter has been airbrushed out of the history of British planning, but it was around his table that a group of extraordinary people were to meet. William Morris was there and so was Prince Peter Kropotkin, whose 1898 book *Fields, Factories and Workshops*[11] is a study on how science and technology could be harnessed to improve human wellbeing. Campaigners for women's rights such as Annie Besant were there, as were union leaders like Ben Tillet and politicians such as Kier Hardie. There were also sociologists such as Patrick Geddes, who was to have a profound effect on the planning movement.

It was perhaps the closest to a 'university of utopia' that Britain has ever produced, and it had a profound impact on the young mining engineer Raymond Unwin, who was building brick terraced houses for miners. Unwin was transformed by his relationship with Carpenter (Fig 1.08), and

Fig 1.08a
Raymond Unwin
1.08b
Edward Carpenter

Unwin's relationship with Carpenter had a profound effect on his thinking and quest to realise utopian ideals.

by Carpenter's influential book *Towards democracy*.[12] Unwin would – along with his design partner, Barry Parker – become one of the key driving forces behind the practical realisation of utopian values in the 19th century. Unwin's personal transformation from building regimented terraces to the Arts and Crafts homes in Letchworth Garden City mirrors a broader social transformation that recognised the importance of not just basic sanitation but also of green spaces, gardens and proper community facilities in building Britain's future.[13]

Ebenezer Howard and the Garden City Vision

The final element in the vibrant mix of utopian thinking that characterised the end of the 19th century was Ebenezer Howard. Howard was a parliamentary clerk, who spent his time recording political debates at Westminster. He had tried his hand as a farmer in the US before he returned to write his seminal work, *To-morrow: a peaceful path to real reform*.[14] Howard's book, like Thomas More's *Utopia*, is one of the landmarks of the utopian tradition.

To-morrow was, above all, a synthesis of many of the key ideas of the time. Howard was influenced by Ruskin, Kropotkin, Morris and Henry George, but managed to combine a visionary sense of how people could live with a key financial measure that would make that vision a reality. The heart of his vision was the idea of the garden city. These new self-contained towns would replace slums with high-quality housing for working people; each house would have a decent garden and generous play space for children. The garden cities would provide for the best blend of town and country, not just allowing access to the natural environment but bringing that environment into the heart of the city. These communities would be surrounded

by a belt of agricultural land, which would provide local food for the population as well as access to the countryside. This union of town and country would encourage healthy communities, not just through physical activity and fresh air but via a healthy social life (as well as sufficient personal space – see Chapter 4). The garden cities would also have integrated transport systems and a strong emphasis on democratic, community governance. Each would provide its own employment, in order to limit commuting. They would be towns 'designed for industry and healthy living; of a size that makes possible a full measure of social life, but not larger; surrounded by a permanent belt of rural land; the whole of the land being in public ownership or held in trust for the community'.[15]

A vision of a sociable city

Howard did not envisage isolated communities. He set out a vision for a garden city that would reach an ideal population of around 32,000 people. Once this planned limit had been reached, a new city would be started a short distance away – followed by another, and another, until a network of such places was created, each connected to the others through excellent public transport, providing all the benefits of a much larger city but with each resident having easy access to the countryside. Howard called this network of connected settlements the 'Social City' (Fig 1.09).

Having taken the overspill population from the crowded larger cities, these existing industrial cities could then be replanned to improve the urban environment. Howard's ambitions were extraordinary:

For the vastness of the task which seems to frighten some of my friends, represents, in fact, the very measure of its value to the community, if that task be only undertaken in a worthy spirit and with worthy aims ... to establish a scientific system of distribution

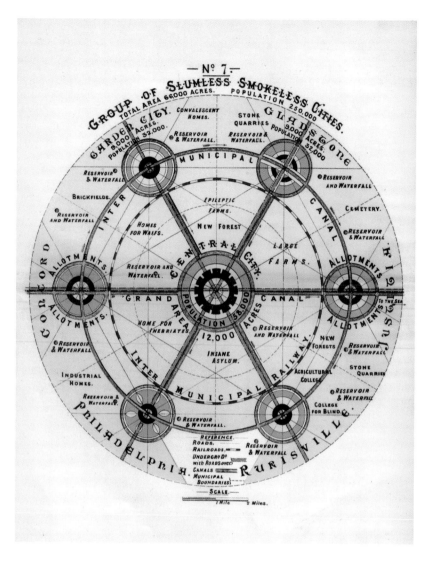

Fig 1.09
Howard envisaged a group of settlements, linked by rapid public transport, together providing the benefits of a much larger city.

to take the place of a chaos, a just system of land tenure for one representing the selfishness which we hope is passing away; to found pensions with liberty for our aged poor, now imprisoned in workhouses; to banish despair and awaken hope in the breasts of those who have fallen; to silence the harsh voice of anger, and to awaken the soft notes of brotherliness and goodwill; to place in strong hands implements of peace and construction, so that implements of war and destruction may drop uselessly down ...[16]

The fundamental idea that underpinned Howard's vision was capturing and redistributing the increase in land values, which development creates, for the long-term benefit of the whole community. This was not a new idea, and in fact has resonance with all those who have argued for fairer distribution of land rights since the 16th century – it is a principle that sits at the heart of the practical realisation of utopia. But its practical effect was to be precisely harnessed in the garden cities, to create a financial model that would not only pay back the loans needed to buy land and build infrastructure but could provide long-term funds to make communities effectively self-sufficient. The question was whether this high ambition could be turned into a practical reality. ◆

chapter 2

THE GARDEN CITIES

Ebenezer Howard's determination to realise his vision resulted in a period of exceptional productivity. In 1899, just a year after To-morrow *was published, the Garden City Association was formed, and in 1903 Howard purchased an estate at Letchworth, Hertfordshire and founded the world's first garden city (Fig 2.01).*

Letchworth: The World's First Garden City

When Howard and his supporters founded Letchworth Garden City, they did not have to concern themselves with local plans or national policy as there was no statutory planning system. In 1902, the Garden City Association (now the Town and Country Planning Association – TCPA) had set up the Garden City Pioneer Company, whose primary role was to find a site. The sites had to be of 1,600–2,400 hectares in size, in a single block; be in private hands; lie near London, or another large city with a suitable rail link; and offer 'economically feasible' water supply and drainage. The process of evaluating the various sites included an assessment by Thomas Adams, the association's secretary, and Raymond Unwin, and the canvassing of manufacturers to ascertain whether they would be willing to move their operations to the new town.

Buying the land required patient investors who were willing to see returns over the medium and long term. The articles of the Pioneer Company limited dividends to 5% and recycled additional profits for community use. The intention was that the company would own the majority of commercial and housing property, collecting revenue from leaseholds that would allow the recouping of rising property values.

Fig 2.01
Letchworth, The Road
by Spencer Gore.

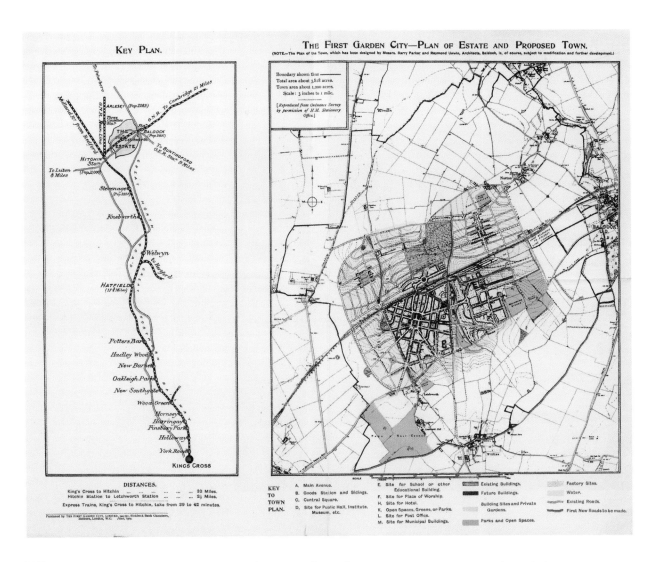

KEY PLAN.

THE FIRST GARDEN CITY—PLAN OF ESTATE AND PROPOSED TOWN.

Fig 2.02
'Town and country must be married' – the 1904 Plan for Letchworth.

Designing the first garden city

The design of Letchworth was initially in the hands of Raymond Unwin and Barry Parker, who translated Howard's ideals in to an innovative masterplan that sought to work with the grain of the landscape[1] (Fig 2.02). The site was some 1,500 hectares, of which 530 hectares were reserved for the town and the rest was agricultural belt to supply it with local food. The city, for 32,000 people, was framed by a strong Ruskinian ethos of design as 'civic art' with a real commitment to beauty, fellowship and cooperative values. Only one tree was felled to create the design. The generosity of green space and preservation of existing natural features and habitats was pioneering, and contributes to Letchworth's continued beauty.

The individual housing designs for Letchworth reflected both the Arts and Crafts aesthetic and, in particular, the inspiration of architects such as Philip Webb and C.F.A. Voysey – alongside an acute awareness of costs. Unwin set out a design guide that specified particular

that dominated working-class housing provision elsewhere. There is now a myth that Unwin set a rigid rule of 12 homes to the acre (just under five per hectare), but in fact he recognised the need for flexibility in provision in central areas. The point was, however, to break down the traditional division between town and country, creating a new kind of place that was both socially inclusive and embedded in the natural environment.

These ideas would have immediate international influence on the rapid urbanisation of North America at the time. Lewis Mumford, Henry Wright and Clarence Stein established the Regional Planning Association of America, effectively the US version of the Garden Cities Association, in 1923. The RPAA translated the garden city design approach to the development of Radburn, New Jersey in 1929 (Fig 2.04). As we explore in Chapter 3, Radburn was to directly influence Britain's new towns movement a century later. There continued a rich UK–US dialogue about large-scale development – recorded in letters exchanged between Lewis Mumford and Frederic Osborn at the Garden Cities Association.[4]

Homes for All

The social ambition of Letchworth stands in stark contrast to 21st-century attitudes to social housing. In essence, high-quality design was for everyone without the startling difference in space and amenity that now scars the housing market. Much of the provision was co-housing, with the ambition for residents to be active self-managers. Cost remained a problem however, and the 1905 Cheap Cottages Exhibition was one attempt to attract innovation in building materials (Fig 2.05).

Soon after its foundation in 1903, Letchworth became famous for its political, cultural and educational innovation. Its early inhabitants tended to be the 'idealistic,

Fig 2.03
Barry Parker's drawing office at Letchworth.

materials – banning slate, for example – but there was also a close, personal relationship between the early planners and architects at Letchworth. There was strong sense of shared endeavour in this Edwardian utopia. The Unwin-and-Parker-designed company office (Fig 2.03) is, perhaps, the best example of the collective, romantic idealism that was so much the legacy of William Morris.

At the heart of many of the housing designs was an attempt to capture the English vernacular tradition of the artisan cottage.[2] Homes were often grouped around 'village greens' with generous gardens, in sharp contrast to the regimented bye-law[3] design

Fig 2.04a /2.04b
Garden City concepts such as groups of homes (seen here at Rushby Walk, Letchworth – a), were translated into the culs de sac of Radburn, New Jersey (b).

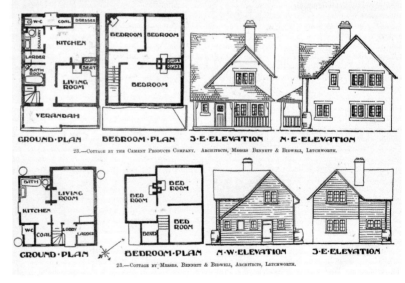

Fig 2.05a /2.05b
Catalogue and plans showing layout of the £150 homes from the Cheap Cottages Exhibition.

artistic middle class, who gave Letchworth
a permanent reputation of crankiness that it
later ill deserved'.[5] However, the garden city
ideals became a mainstream part of national
political debate, with cross-party supporters.
1909 saw Britain's first town-planning act,
which gave local government limited powers
to prepare plans coming into force and saw
the beginnings of the professionalisation of
town planning. Local-government planning
powers remained weak and, crucially, they
had little control over land use because
of the risk of paying compensation to
landowners. Other private experiments
applied aspects of garden city ideals in
design and management – most notably,
Parker and Unwin's proposals for Hampstead
Garden Suburb for the social reformer and
National Trust founder, Henrietta Barnett
(Fig 2.06).

Fig 2.06a / 2.06b
In 1906, Parker and Unwin
were appointed to design a
'Garden Suburb' for London,
sparking an ongoing debate
about the role of different
scales of 'Garden Settlement'.

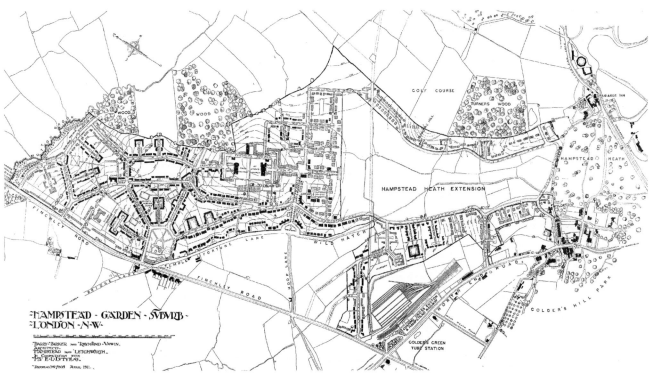

HAMPSTEAD · GARDEN · SUBURB ·
LONDON · N·W·

BARRY · PARKER AND RAYMOND · UNWIN ·
ARCHITECTS ·
HAMPSTEAD AND LETCHWORTH ·
IN CONSULTATION WITH
Mr · E·L·LVTYENS ·
DRAWING N° / 503 · APRIL 1911 ·

There were certainly major problems in finding investors for Letchworth, and concerns as early as 1905 that some of Howard's fellow trustees did not share his high social ambition – particularly for residents' self-government.[6] It is also impossible to know how far the garden cities would have progressed had it not been for the outbreak of the first world war. Letchworth had only 10 years to develop before activity was effectively halted.

Even so, the movement had begun to have international impact, with garden city inspired communities across Europe – from the suburbs of Paris to Poland, and even further afield to South Africa and South America.[7] Notable examples include Hellerau in Dresden, Germany (Fig 2.07) and the suburbs of Sao Paulo, designed by Raymond Unwin. The Garden Cities Association ran frequent study tours to such developments (Fig 2.08), and by 1916 was receiving so much international interest (over 200 requests for advice a month at one point)[8] that it founded the International Garden Cities Association to promote garden cities worldwide.[9] The flow of learning ran both ways, with international examples having a clear influence on the evolution of large-scale development in the UK.[10]

The Impact of the First World War

The first world war did not just have a practical effect on curtailing development at Letchworth; it had a profound political and psychological impact on the utopians, undermining the credibility of ideals based on cooperation and human fellowship.[11] The end of the war was marked by one the most famous political promises of modern British history: 'Homes Fit for Heroes'. David Lloyd George's government did introduce new housing standards championed by Raymond Unwin, by now an influential

Fig 2.07
Hellerau, Dresden, was designed in 1909 and inspired by the Garden City movement.

Fig 2.08
The Garden City movement received instant international interest and the Association has a long history of international study tours – like this to Gothenburg in 1947.

23

member of the Tudor Walters Committee whose recommendations set standards for council-house design. Local-government bodies received new powers and new money to build working-class housing to an unprecedentedly high standard. There was funding for the back-to-the-land smallholding movement, with some councils buying farms to rent to returning servicemen. There was also a massive expansion in private-sector housing, often copying the design features of the Arts and Crafts tradition and even claiming to be 'garden suburbs'. 1919 held great promise, not least to returning serviceman; the question for politicians was whether they would sustain their commitment to build homes fit for heroes in the worsening postwar economic environment. In the end, it proved to be a promise only half fulfilled.

The interwar period was one of deep frustration for the garden city movement. Many of its ideas had been taken up in housing design and layout – particularly in large London County Council estates, which experienced a transformation in housing standards. There had been much less success, however, with the wider project of place-making. Municipal planning remained very weak, and the garden city pioneers' pursuit of a mutualised development model remained the exception rather than the rule. Vast tracts of suburban housing appeared along London's arterial roads that aped the garden city housing designs while ignoring every one of their key place-making principles.

The 1930s – utopia delayed

While one should not downplay the level of genuine achievement that the garden cities inspired in the UK and internationally, it was not all what Howard had hoped for. Letchworth itself struggled from being undercapitalised, which meant that its development company, First Garden City Limited, was unable to build at the rate it had intended. Shareholders committed to limited dividends as per Howard's model, but would not see a return for much longer than anticipated. It was, somewhat ironically, an income boost from interwar public-sector housebuilding programmes that changed Letchworth's fortunes (through investment from public sector housebuilding programmes) and allowed building to accelerate.

By the late 1950s, Letchworth became so profitable that it was subject to a takeover bid by property speculators. Saved by an act of parliament, its future was secured and the assets of First Garden City Ltd transferred to a public-sector organisation, the Letchworth Garden City Corporation. In 1995, another act of parliament saw the establishment of a body – the Letchworth Garden City Heritage Foundation – to look after the town. The foundation was endowed with the £56m Letchworth Estate. Through the stewardship of the foundation, £4m is reinvested in the town every year via 'charitable initiatives'. On the ground, this means investment in everything from a cinema and arts facilities to a local health service and Christmas dinners for the elderly. The foundation operates a 'Scheme of Management', which means that all freehold properties in its estate must comply with a scheme designed to maintain the garden city's aesthetic. In practice, this means restrictions on things like cutting down trees or paving over front gardens.[12] By accident or design, Letchworth is today home to 33,000 people – not far off the figure envisaged by Howard. Around a third (31%) of housing in Letchworth is socially rented.[13]

Welwyn Garden City – Howard's Second Experiment

After the first world war, Howard began work on a new garden city project at Welwyn, Hertfordshire – this time with the involvement of the accountant Charles Purdom and Frederic Osborn, who had already promoted garden cities with Howard and who would become instrumental in the campaign for garden cities and the postwar new towns programme. Having persuaded the then chair of the Garden Cities and Town Planning Association to raise a £500 deposit, on 30 May 1919, Howard bought 600 hectares of land at Welwyn for £51,000 (approximately £184,000 in today's money) 'without the cash to pay for it'.

Second Garden City Ltd was registered on 15 October 1919 in the midst of a wider economic slowdown, and suffered a similarly challenging start to that of its predecesor. It benefitted from the experience at Letchworth and had a more cautious approach to financing, appointing an experienced property magnate as chair and limiting further the dividends to shareholders. Income was to be earned from residential and commercial leaseholders and from the company's various subsidiary operations (everything from brickmakers to bakers and a cooperative store).

Luck, however, was not on Welwyn's side, and just eight years after its founding it fell victim to the worldwide financial crash and subsequent economic depression. By the early 1930s and without government support, the company was in financial trouble, and the directors changed the memorandum and articles to exclude the garden city and its inhabitants from any future profits from the development or company – an abandonment of the fundamental financial principle of Howard's vision that he was, perhaps mercifully, no longer alive to witness.

In fact, the company's position soon reverted to profitability, and by the time Welwyn was designated as a new town, in 1948, it was in a position to purchase additional land and make a bid to expand. The government minister concerned had other ideas, believing that a private company could not be working wholly in the public interest. The company's assets were sold to the new Welwyn Garden City Development Corporation (which shared its staff with Hatfield Development Corporation – designated at the same time). When the corporation was wound up, with it went the assets earned by the development company and corporation, and Welwyn became like any other new town in terms of its finances.

Designing Welwyn Garden City

Frederic Osborn drafted initial ideas for the new garden city, incorporated into a masterplan by C.M. Crickmer, who had worked previously at Letchworth. However, the plan did not meet approval, and so Second Garden City Ltd turned to the RIBA for an architect. Louis de Soissons, a Canadian practitioner, became chief architect for the garden city (all designs passed by his desk) until his death in 1962. De Soissons was heavily influenced by Parker and Unwin, and his layout for the garden city reflected this with groups of homes, generous green space and zoning of industrial areas, along with other contemporary influences such as the Parisian trend for axial roads. The masterplan (Fig 2.09) was laid out on two axes – one parallel to the railway line and another, perpendicular one leading to the station – all complemented by sweeping lines. De Soissons' interpretation of the neo-Georgian aesthetic provided a vernacular for the garden city's buildings, sitting proudly along these axial routes.

Fig 2.09
Welwyn was Howard's
second experiment in
applying garden city
principles.

The plan would continue to influence the development of Welwyn when it was designated a new town.

Today, Welwyn has a population of around 47,000.[14] It is regarded by many as the prettier of the two garden cities and has managed to maintain these good looks through a Scheme of Management, whereby anyone wanting to make alterations to the look of the exterior of their home or front garden has to adhere to a set of clear principles (Fig 2.10). Welwyn is the only place in England that has such a scheme run by the local authority rather than a charitable trust. This is a massive financial burden on the authority, which, unlike Letchworth's foundation, does not have an income source to pay for it. As Welwyn is also under pressure for development, the council has to decide to what extent it should be allowed to grow and the role of garden city principles in this process.

Lessons From the Garden Cities

The world today looks very different to that of 1903, but we still face many of the issues that Howard and his supporters confronted: a chronic undersupply of housing, overcrowding and unhealthy living conditions in many of our cities. These issued are explored in Chapter 5, but for now it is worth reflecting on the lessons provided by the garden city model and the Garden City Association's attempts to make that model a reality at Letchworth and Welwyn.

Fig 2.10
Welwyn Garden City today – its Scheme of Management maintains some control of the streetscape.

Fig 2.11
Howard Park, Letchworth –
by recycling the profits of land
ownership, the Letchworth
Garden City Heritage
Foundation is able to invest
in well-managed parks and
greenspace.

These lessons provide a wealth of learning about how to develop new communities today, which can be distilled into four broad but interrelated principles (Box 2.01).

Fig 2.12
Worker's cottages in Letchworth - the town was designed to provide affordable homes for everyone, and homes of all tenures were afforded the same quality of design and materials.

> *Box 2.01: Learning from the garden cities – key principles for building new communities today*
>
> 1. Take a long-term, holistic approach.
>
> 2. Spatial patterns of growth matter – towns must have a 'stop'.
>
> 3. Ensure that the profits from development benefit everyone.
>
> 4. Nurture social sustainability through meaningful public participation and long-term stewardship.

Take a long-term, holistic approach

The garden cities were designed to be places of beauty that would lift the spirits of those who lived in them. It is therefore not surprising that they have stood the test of time and, though they have their critics, remain popular places to live more than a century later. Parker's and Unwin's Arts and Crafts homes and De Soissons' neo-Georgian villas were built to provide genuinely affordable homes for everyone. Market forces mean that today many of the privately owned original properties are unaffordable for the majority – but this demonstrates the benefits of an emphasis on quality and craftsmanship, and how putting people's needs at the centre of the design process has meant that homes have been adaptable to changing needs and have remained attractive places to live for generations. Their landscape setting of open spaces, parks, tree-lined streets and private gardens – much replicated in countless developments worldwide – was integral to the earliest stages of design. In this 'multifunctional landscape' setting, walkable neighbourhoods, the early provision of arts and cultural facilities, and local jobs and amenities were all designed to work together, to facilitate healthy and sociable lives. Quite simply, design that puts people before profit; uses quality materials, with attention to detail; takes a 'whole-place' approach; and embeds landscape, nature, culture and the arts has a clear impact on wellbeing and the longevity of place (Fig 2.11). While most of these ideas are now embedded in good urban-design practice, the reality of many modern housing developments is quite the opposite – often leading to developments that not only encourage long-distance commuting or provide the smallest living spaces in Europe, but which are likely to require demolition in 30 years' time as demographics, and therefore household requirements, change and poor-quality materials fail (Fig 2.12).

Spatial patterns of growth matter – 'towns must have a stop'

Howard's vision of a series of connected cities surrounded by agricultural belt providing food and access to nature has influenced the town and country planning system, and has left a visual legacy across the UK's landscape. His concept of avoiding endlessly sprawling cities by creating instead a series of linked new settlements was later articulated by Sir Frederic Osborn in the phrase 'towns must have a stop'.[15] The basis of this idea was that while it may appear to be politically or economically more efficient to add another housing estate, suburb, 'Sustainable Urban Extension' or business park to an existing town, that town must eventually reach its limit. The limit might be a physical one – a waterfront or railway line, for example – or it might just be the sense that the latest expansion of the town is 'so removed from the heart of the place that it might not be part of the place at all'.[16] The garden cities were designed to be the antithesis of suburban sprawl, an idea that would later

result in a national green-belt policy aiming not only to prevent sprawl and coalescence but also to protect the setting of historic towns and safeguard the countryside. Though there is a very lively debate on the role of the green belt in Britain, and a clear need to reform how it is used (to encourage greater access and local food, and to better consider its role in climate-change adaptation and energy generation, for example), we only need look at US cities to see the consequences of a lack of urban-containment policy and unregulated urban sprawl (Fig 2.13).

Ensure that the profits from development benefit everyone

What was really revolutionary about Howard's model was that the residents of the garden city would share in the profits of the development process. Today, land increases in value not only when it is built on but when it is granted planning permission (this is known as betterment). At present, while some of this land-value increase is promised to the local authority, through impact fees such as those embodied in Section 106 agreements and the Community Infrastructure Levy, the vast majority goes to the (usually private-sector) landowner. The importance of this in paying for future garden cities is explained further in Chapter 6, but this remains the single most powerful lesson from the garden cities movement. Its financial model provided the means necessary to look after the garden city in perpetuity. The vastly different fates of the two built examples demonstrate this clearly. What council today wouldn't want a body looking after its town and cities without a cost to the public purse? What the experience of the garden cities at Letchworth and Welwyn tell us is not only that there must be sufficient up-front capital to pay for infrastructure but also that there has to be some form of legal or 'constitutional' commitment to sharing development profits, to ensure that the model works in perpetuity.

Nurture social sustainability through meaningful public participation and long-term stewardship

Howard's vision for a 'cooperative commonwealth' meant that residents of the garden city would not only share in the profits of development but would also have a participative role in the governance and development of the place. Although the opportunities for inhabitants to benefit from the profits of the development process, as set out in Howard's vision, were diluted in both the garden city experiments, in both cases the development companies put huge effort into creating lively and sociable towns that people would enjoy living in from the outset. For example, the cooperative stores at Welwyn (Fig 2.14) and Welwyn Builders and Joiners Ltd (a subsidiary of the original development company) provided an opportunity for

Fig 2.14
Welwyn stores was one of many cooperative companies set up; today, appropriately, the site is occupied by John Lewis.

Fig 2.15
The Letchworth pioneers linked nature and place-making, and involved the public in development; here children are planting mature specimen trees for Letchworth's first Arbor Day.

people to have a stake in local economic initiatives. In both garden cities, up-front investment was made in a whole range of artistic and cultural facilities and groups, such as theatrical societies and youth clubs, which set them apart from other developments at the time. Today, the benefits of social and cultural development for health and wellbeing are well understood, but the garden cities were among the first to show what is possible if people have an active role in community life (Fig 2.15). Subsequent experience has emphasised the importance of the stewardship provided by the garden city development companies, and the important role of meaningful public engagement in both process and governance.

A Nation on the Edge of Change

By 1940, key pioneers like Howard and Unwin had passed away. However, the sacrifice of the second world war, and a country in need of a brave new future, was to be a catalyst for the garden city ideals to enter mainstream political thinking and underpin the quest for a new utopia: out of the ashes of conflict, the new towns programme was born. ◆

chapter 3

NEW TOWN UTOPIA

While the garden cities had shown it was possible to find a new way to live, the devastation of the second world war brought with it the realisation that the entire nation deserved a new future. This chapter looks at the conditions in which communities were living in the postwar period, and the ambition and evolution of the new towns programme from the 1940s through to the end of the 20th century. It explores the new town designation process and the key delivery vehicles, the new town development corporations; how they were funded; some of the common characteristics shared by all new towns, and what it was like to be a new town resident.

Postwar Britain

Following the war, overcrowding and slums remained rife throughout Britain's inner cities. Entire families could be found living in single rooms in terraces or courts, often dimly lit and without proper ventilation or sanitation. Bomb damage had destroyed thousands of homes, and six years' of potential housebuilding had been lost. As servicemen returned and families began to rebuild their lives, the Labour Government achieved a landslide victory, reflecting the nation's desire for change. A programme of new towns would be visible proof of the government's pledge to 'build a new society on the ruins of the old' (Fig 3.01).[1]

In 1946, the New Towns Act was introduced, crowning 60 years of political agitation for decent planning. Introducing the legislation in parliament, the town planning minister Lewis Silkin quoted Thomas More's *Utopia*. It would seem inconceivable to invoke that heritage now, but at the time it was part of a long and honourable tradition of radical approaches to land and communities.

The new towns programme would lead to the designation of 32 new towns over a period of 50 years, providing homes and jobs for over 2.8 million people in 'balanced communities' – a scheme of planned urban development that has not been rivalled since. But, as we will see, the dream was cut short, and we would later learn that there was a price to pay for delivering at such speed and in a time of austerity. Nevertheless, it provided many lessons in place-making from which we still have much to learn.

Fig 3.01
The Labour Party was keen to show the action it would take on housing.

Osborn's Patient Campaign

The case for a programme of new towns was actually made in the decade preceding the war. By the mid-1930s, the Garden Cities & Town Planning Association (GCTPA) was increasingly frustrated with the slow progress in housebuilding (including at Letchworth and Welwyn) and felt that there was clearly the need for a comprehensive, strategic approach to considering the nation's housing needs. As councils focused on building endless housing estates – often borrowing the

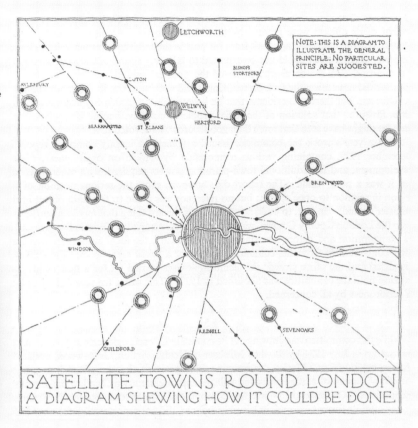

Fig 3.03
The Garden Cities & Town Planning Association's vision for satellite towns around London in 1920 – over 20 years before Abercrombie's Greater London Plan suggested the same solution.

NOTE: THIS IS A DIAGRAM TO ILLUSTRATE THE GENERAL PRINCIPLE. NO PARTICULAR SITES ARE SUGGESTED.

SATELLITE TOWNS ROUND LONDON
A DIAGRAM SHEWING HOW IT COULD BE DONE.

Fig 3.02
If Ebenezer Howard was the father of the Garden City movement, then Frederic Osborn was the father of the New Towns programme.

garden city aesthetic, but without the jobs and facilities to accompany the homes – new communities were out of favour. This did not deter the GCTPA which – led by Frederic J. Osborn (Fig 3.02), the organisation's secretary – demanded a more strategic approach. This included campaigning for regional planning, forming alliances with other organisations and also submitting very influential evidence supporting this strategic approach to a succession of bodies, not least the Barlow Commission on the geographical distribution of the industrial population.[2] The report of the commission concluded that large cites were a problem and that it was necessary to plan for homes and jobs outside them.

Even in wartime, the government could not ignore the evidence before it. With support from both of the main British political parties, Patrick Abercrombie – an internationally renowned architect–planner – published the Greater London Plan[3] in 1944, which would set the framework for the decentralisation of London's population and would become the basis for a national plan for housebuilding.[4] Inner-city slums would be demolished and replaced with modern housing estates, while a ring of satellite towns around London would provide new homes and jobs (an idea proposed by TCPA over 20 years previously, see Fig 3.03). The scene was set for radical action following the war.

Before we build—

—a plan

We all know that in Britain today there are towns that suffer from overcrowding and lack of planning. The twofold purpose of the Ministry of Town and Country Planning is to improve existing conditions wherever possible and to ensure that order and beauty shall come to our towns and cities of the future. These pictures show what intelligent planning can do and what it tries to avoid.

Fig 3.04
Planning poster, showing how the 1947 Town and Country Planning Act would transform the land-use and development system for generations to come.

Planning the New Towns

There followed a period of intense activity to make this vision a reality. Following his appointment in 1945, the new minister of town and country planning, Lewis Silkin, appointed Lord Reith to chair a New Towns Committee (later known as the Reith Committee). Within 12 months, the committee had published three succinct but detailed, and profoundly influential, reports on how to deliver a programme of new towns – covering everything from open space to management arrangements. The ink was barely dry on the final report when, in 1946, the New Towns Act was passed, providing the tools to make the programme a reality. The legislation detailed how the series of large-scale new towns would be located and paid for, and how they would be planned and delivered by dedicated single-purpose, long-life organisations called development corporations, appointed by the government.

The New Towns Act 1946 was part of a postwar settlement, which, along with the Town and Country Planning Act 1947 (which introduced the planning system), instituted the nationalisation of the right to develop land, the capture of land values generated by the grant of planning permission (known as betterment), and a reformed system of statutory development-plan making by local authorities.[5] Never before had Britain seen a government with such an ambitious programme to provide high-quality housing in well-designed communities as part of a wider public programme addressing public health and social justice.[6] Public-information films and posters (Figs 3.04 and 3.05) explained to the populace what a different their new utopia might make.

Lewis Silkin himself had far from modest ambitions for the new towns and the opportunity they presented to build a better future for the nation. His philosophy would guide the approach to delivery:

Our aim must be to combine in the new town the friendly spirit of the former slum with the vastly improved health conditions of the new estate, but it must be a broadened spirit, embracing all classes of society … We may well produce in the new towns a new type of citizen, a healthy, self-respecting dignified person with a sense of beauty, culture and civic pride.[7]

Fig 3.05
The government used public information films like 'Charlie in New Town' to excite the public about the new towns project.

Finding sites for the new towns

Like the New Towns Committee, Silkin and his team did not hesitate to get this project underway. In November 1946, just three months after the New Towns Act was passed, the first new town was designated at Stevenage. Between 1946 and 1970, 33 new towns were designated across the United Kingdom (including Stonehouse near Glasgow, which was later abandoned).

The programme was delivered in three phases:

▸ **'Mark One'**
designated between 1946 and 1950;

▸ **'Mark Two'**
designated between 1961 and 1966; and

▸ **'Mark Three'**
designated between 1967 and 1970.

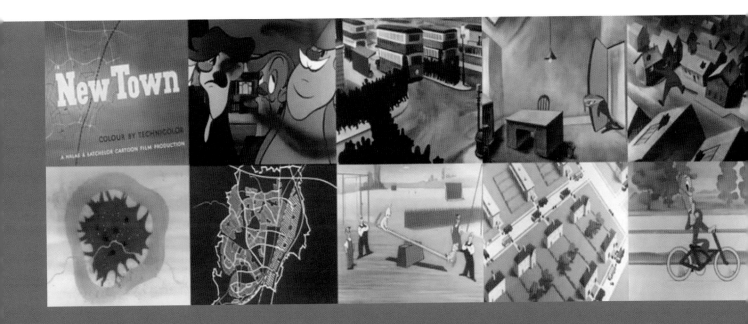

New Towns
● 'Mark One'
● 'Mark Two'
● 'Mark Three'
● Letchworth Garden City
'46 Designation date

Glenrothes '48
Cumbernauld '55
Livingston '62
East Kilbride '47
Irvine '66

Derry-Londonderry '69
Ballymena '67
Antrim '66
Craigavon '65

Washington '64
Peterlee '48
Newton Aycliffe '47

Central Lancashire '70
Skelmersdale '61
Warrington '68
Runcorn '64

Telford '63
Peterborough '67
Corby '50
Newtown '67
Northampton '68
Redditch '64
Letchworth Garden City '03
Milton Keynes '67
Stevenage '46
Welwyn Garden City '48 (Garden City '19)
Cwmbran '49
Hemel Hempstead '47
Harlow '47
Hatfield '48
Basildon '49
Bracknell '49
Crawley '47

Fig 3.06
Map showing the locations
and designation dates of the UK's
32 New Towns plus Letchworth
and Welwyn Garden City.

Of these 32 realised new towns, 21 were in England, 2 in Wales, 5 in Scotland and four in Northern Ireland (Fig 3.06).

Contrary to common assumptions, identifying the locations for many of the new towns was a local-authority-led process (Fig 3.07). The Mark One new towns were designated to provide homes for Londoners, and as overspill from Birmingham. Patrick Abercrombie's 1944 Greater London Plan had provided areas of search for a ring of satellite towns around London to serve this purpose. Regional or sub-regional studies were also conducted for other major cities or conurbations that were suffering from chronic overcrowding and poor living conditions – notably Belfast, Glasgow and Greater Merseyside. The South Wales Plan explored the opportunities for using the new towns legislation in Wales. Other new towns, such as Peterlee and Milton Keynes, were voluntary proposals from county councils who were keen to address development issues in their area.

New town development corporations

Like the garden city development companies that preceded them, the new town development corporations were dedicated delivery bodies working for the public good in a quest for healthy, socially balanced communities. But unlike the garden cities cases, these would be public bodies with government-endowed planning and borrowing powers enabling them to fulfil the wide remit of doing 'everything necessary to deliver the town'.[8] No town-building body since has rivalled the scope of the new town development corporations. The New Towns Act 1946 set out their core powers (see Box 3.01).

Box 3.01: Objects and powers of new town development corporations

▶ the power to compulsory purchase land if it could not be bought by voluntary agreement;

▶ the power to buy land at current-use value (later, after the Myers legal ruling,[9] some 'hope value' – ie the value that might be created by the 'hope' of future development – also had to be paid) and capture the betterment for the Treasury (and thus, ultimately, the public);

▶ the power to borrow money (primarily from the Treasury), repayable with interest;

▶ the power to prepare a masterplan, which, after public inquiry and approval by the minister, would be the statutory development plan;

▶ the power to grant or refuse planning permission for development within the new town designated area (with certain small exceptions, although local 'partnership' agreements sometimes extended that range so long as they helped in the mission to deliver the new town);

▶ the power to procure housing subsidised by central government grant and by other means, and to act as a housing association in the management of housing; and

▶ the power to do anything necessary for the development of the town, such as undertaking the delivery of utilities or entering into partnership working with other agencies, investing in social and community development, promoting local economic development and marketing the new town overseas.

Fig 3.07
One of the key misconceptions about the New Towns programme was that the locations were decided centrally - in fact, it was often a local authority-led process.

"It's not fair. I want to throw for Satellite Towns in 1949. You picked them all last year"

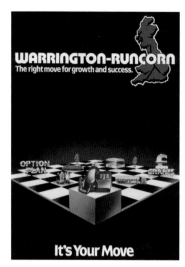

Fig 3.08a-d
Promotional materials, such as these brochures for Warrington and Runcorn new towns, were an essential tool for attracting investment at home and abroad.

The creation of 'balanced communities' referred not just to housing but also to investment in social development and a strong employment base. The corporations were marketing 'machines', travelling worldwide to attract employers to their new towns, able to offer homes for employees as well as affordable land (Fig 3.08). The relative autonomy of the corporations was also key to their success. They had clearance to 'do the deals' necessary to get development moving. This combination of power and resources meant speedy delivery of development. It also meant, in many cases, complicated relationships with local authorities, who were sometimes jealous of the corporations operating in their 'patch'.

Designing the New Towns

The design ethos of the new towns was not simply to provide homes and jobs but also to create socially balanced communities that integrated employment, homes and social life to provide opportunities for all. The minister encouraged the corporations to be 'daring and courageous in their efforts to discover the best way of living'.[10] With central-government funding, the corporations were able to attract the best young design talent from across the UK and continental Europe (Fig 3.09).

While the design characteristics of the garden cities had been heavily influenced by the Arts and Crafts movement, those of the new towns were substantially shaped by Modernism, interpreted in a way that aimed to retain the garden city vision of marrying town and country. It was in the new towns that the goals of the garden city and Modernist movements were united – for the former, in terms of town planning; for the latter, in terms of architecture.[11]

The new town designs were also influenced by the evolution of architecture and design thinking across the world – but, most notably and directly, were the result of an

Fig 3.09
Milton Keynes Development
Corporation (MKDC) in 1975;
the development corporations
attracted the best young talent
and provided dedicated teams
for the town-building task.

Fig 3.10/3.10b
Radburn (a) separated vehicle and pedestrian movement, using greenspace to connect networks of walkways-providing space for children to play on communal areas in front of houses. This gave a perception of healthier and safer spaces, and clearly influenced the layout of Glenrothes (b).

important UK–US dialogue on planning and design. The American urbanist Clarence Perry had developed the concept of 'neighbourhood units', taking inspiration directly from Parker's and Unwin's designs, wherein key amenities were located a short walking distance from homes and at a scale that encouraged social interaction and a sense of place. Perry's concept included self-contained neighbourhood units consisting of culs-de-sac, surrounded by major roads with shops at the edge and a school at the centre – exemplified by the development at Radburn, New Jersey (Fig 3.10a). Radburn, by the architect-planner Clarence Stein, had introduced a new design principle – the separation of vehicles and pedestrian-movement networks. This approach had been recommended by Patrick Abercrombie in the Greater London Plan and in the Dudley Report on the design of dwellings in 1944. The idea, enshrined in these reports, that housing should be laid out in a planned way to provide for a better quality of life formed new consensus in Britain's urban design during this postwar period (Fig 3.10b).

Two important changes to Stein's approach had an impact on how the new towns developed, however. First, new town homes were terraces rather than detached villas. Second, garages were grouped into courts – often a short distance away from homes, with poor surveillance. As a consequence, many homes had poorly identifiable fronts and backs. People would often use the back door – closer to their car – thus removing activity from the street in front of homes. Such characteristics continue to be visible in many contemporary developments.

New town masterplans

The new towns followed the garden city tradition of development by masterplan (Fig 3.11). This holistic approach allowed their corporations to think strategically about how design and layout would help

Fig 3.11a/3.11b
Helmut Jacoby's 1976
vision of central Milton Keynes
(a) seen beside central Milton
Keynes today
(b) illustrate the power of
a strong masterplan.

or hinder their goal of creating 'balanced communities'. A layout plan would be accompanied by a series of supporting documents on specific issues, such as water or green space – much like today's practice.

The designers of the first-wave new towns, often fresh from the armed forces, created rigid blueprints for development, which provided little flexibility for change over the long lifetime of a new community. Later, new towns learnt from this experience and recognised that the most effective approach was to create a framework for development, which was strong enough to guide future patterns but flexible enough to allow for innovation over time: 'a trellis on which the roses can grow where they will'.[12]

These masterplans still guide future development in many of the new towns, and in many cases provided a valuable framework for councils to continue the job of the development corporations when the latter were prematurely wound up.

Walkable neighbourhoods with a range of local community facilities, set within a comprehensive framework of green infrastructure, had been promoted by the garden city pioneers, and was developed further through the new towns. These principles have now been embedded as good practice in urban design.

Common design characteristics

Design varied, of course, from place to place and between different periods of development. However, in many cases designers moved from one development corporation to another, taking their design approaches with them, and it is possible to identify a number of characteristics that are recognisable across many of the new towns:

Neighbourhood units

Influenced by the garden cities and, later, Radburn, housing was developed in 'neighbourhood units', built around a

primary school and other local facilities, creating a sense of community and allowing people to be within a short walk of key facilities. This was intended to reinforce local identity and serve day-to-day needs, with the town centre providing larger facilities.

Low density

A combination of relatively cheap land, emphasis on green space and recognition that high-rise development did not necessarily equate to healthy living conditions meant that the new towns were built at low densities. At Harlow, this was as low as four dwellings per hectare in some places.

Zoning of industrial and residential areas

First envisaged by the garden city pioneers to separate housing from the polluting noise, smells and traffic of industry, housing and industrial areas were separated in the new towns. Excellent pedestrian and transport links encouraged people to walk to work or take public transport.

Pedestrian-friendly town centres

Pedestrianised town centres – in the first generation – and covered shopping malls – in the later new town centres – not only allowed for a safe and pleasant environment for commercial activity, but was also intended to emphasise the public space between buildings and the social life and positive environment that can thereby be created. This was consciously a radical departure from the traditional high street, where traffic went through town centres rather than around them. It was a feature envisaged earlier by Ebenezer Howard and later influenced by design in Sweden (eg in the 1950s' new town of Vällingby[13]) and the United States (eg early examples in Ohio, Seattle and Illinois).

Ease of movement

Pedestrians and vehicles were often separated into different networks – allowing people to move freely and safely from place to place, with underpasses and overpasses making it unnecessary to cross busy roads. This also allowed for rapid movement by public transport and private car. The natural layout to achieve this was a grid (Figs 3.12–14).

Integrated green infrastructure network

The new towns continued the garden city tradition of combining town and country, using networks of green space throughout their masterplans. These ran along transport corridors, to ease movement for pedestrians and cyclists and to separate transport from the neighbourhood units

Fig 3.12
Runcorn's iconic 'figure of 8' busway was designed to connect residential and commercial areas, and meant that nearly every home was no more than five minutes from a bus stop.

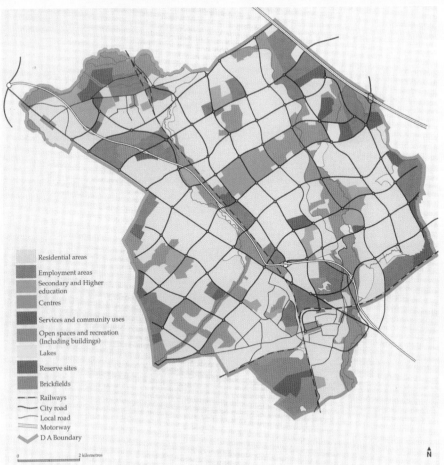

Fig 3.13
Underpasses are a common feature in many of the new towns and were designed to separate traffic and pedestrians.

Fig 3.14
The 1967 Masterplan for Milton Keynes – the grid provides a network of landscape, public transport and car movements.

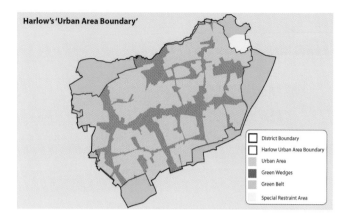

Harlow's 'Urban Area Boundary'

District Boundary
Harlow Urban Area Boundary
Urban Area
Green Wedges
Green Belt
Special Restraint Area

Fig 3.15
When designing Harlow in 1947, Sir Frederick Gibberd aimed to ensure that the existing landscape of the area was respected - hence, the towns iconic 'Green Wedges'.

Fig 3.16
Housing in Cumbernauld, East Lothian c. 1967 - dsigned to provide close proximity to play and green space, as echoed by modern Scandinavian design.

through parks and 'green wedges' (Fig 3.15). They provided access to green space throughout the town – including in formal and informal parks, and neighbourhoods at densities that allowed for green verges and front gardens (Fig 3.16). Following the introduction of the concept in Patrick Abercrombie's Greater London Plan and, later, the Clyde Valley Plan, the Reith Committee recommended a green belt around each of the new towns to prevent them from sprawling and to help realise Howard's vision of towns surrounded by a belt of open country for agriculture and access to countryside – as at Letchworth and Welwyn. But at designation, the requirement for an agricultural green belt was lost, and no new town masterplan has a fixed perimeter of agricultural land – a significant departure from Howard's idea, and a weakness.

Innovative architecture and design

Architects were encouraged to be innovative and use the latest materials, and the development corporations often employed artists to create public art and sometimes to design whole housing estates. Examples include the visionary architectural practice Archigram in Milton Keynes and Victor Pasmore at Peterlee (Fig 3.17). Young architects were keen to prove their worth but were often under unrealistic pressures to build at speed, and some later attracted criticism for allegedly putting design aesthetics before the needs of residents. The new towns also pioneered sustainable-design innovations through initiatives such as Energy World in Milton Keynes.[14] Many of the housing designs wouldn't look out of place in modern Freiburg or Malmö (Fig 3.18).

Emphasis on social housing

The early new towns were dominated by housing that their development corporations built and then rented out as landlords. Between 69% (at Basildon) and 97% (at Peterlee) of housing in the Mark One new towns was for social rent.[15] Such

housing was subsequently transferred to local authorities or housing associations. The later new towns had a more diverse housing-tenure mix, but still included a significant proportion of housing for social rent.

Self-containment

The new towns aimed to be as 'self-contained' as possible (to avoid the creation of commuter suburbs), in that sufficient homes and facilities were to be provided to enable new residents to work and live within the town itself. This approach included industrial strategies that, for several of the early new towns, dictated that people could only move there if they were going to be employed there. In practice, self-containment was a nearly impossible objective, as everywhere has a daily flow of people in and out for various purposes. The new towns were, in reality, part of a network of linked new settlements.

Fig 3.17
Apollo Pavillion, Peterlee – a Victor Pasmore sculpture linking two parts of an estate.

Fig 3.18
Solar house by Dominic Michaelis Associates at the 1981 Homeworld Exhibition, Milton Keynes.

Fig 3.19
Civic art was integral to Gibberd's vision for Harlow, which boasts over 65 public sculptures, many of international signficance: here, a Henry Moore.

47

Space for social and community development

Provision for social and community development included locating community facilities within a short walking distance of homes and designing multifunctional spaces (a school doubling up as a community centre, for example). The development corporations also made a conscious effort to encourage participation in the arts as part of community development. This strength can be seen in all three 'waves' of new towns (Figs 3.19 and 3.20).

Living in the New Towns

The new towns programme was pioneering not only in the scale of its ambition but in the spirit of the earliest new town settlers. These people moved from the inner cities, attracted by the prospect of affordable, modern housing; work; and a better quality of life. The pleasure of newcomers who had never had an inside toilet or separate bedrooms for their children is well documented [16] – as is, conversely, the feeling of isolation that can result from being the first residents of a community. The 'new town blues' were particularly felt by those (mainly women) who had followed their partners to a new life and work in the early new towns, but had been removed

Fig 3.20
Town artists played a prominent role in the later new towns – a library mural by Boyd & Evans, artists in residence at Milton Keynes.

from their social networks and lacked the facilities to meet other people. To counteract this, development corporations invested in people and activities to welcome new residents. Community centres were set up in homes (Fig 3.21) and residents offered a welcome pack, with someone employed specifically to make people feel at home and facilitate social gatherings. The corporations' investments in social and community development is perhaps one of the most impressive legacies of the new towns programme. Everything, from high proportions of social housing to ensuring play facilities were installed ahead of families moving in, was designed to foster social development from the outset. Public art was often a key feature, providing a sense of place and a varied public realm.

Fig 3.21
Community House in Milton Keynes – the corporations worked hard to create a sense of communtiy for the 'pioneer' residents.

Public engagement

There were some commonly raised objections to new town designations; they included concerns of the relevant local authorities over the competitive impact on retail and economic activity in nearby towns, disquiet over the impact on local services, and concerns about the effects on local agricultural economies. Later new towns put specific effort into considering the views of residents: as part of the process of developing the masterplan for Milton Keynes, the consultant planners Llewelyn-Davies, Weeks, Forestier-Walker and Bor undertook a survey of residents living in the villages within the potential designated area of the new town. Annual surveys of new residents' views were also conducted by the development corporation. These included opinions on everything from the design of homes to whether 'housewives' felt they had enough employment opportunities.

Paying for the New Towns

Unlike the privately funded garden cities, the new towns were underpinned by long-term government investment. The New Towns Act introduced borrowing powers for development corporations alongside planning powers. The cost of the new towns programme has become somewhat mythologised, and complicated by the politics and management of policy over time. In fact, the programme remains the UK's primary example of the long-term financial and societal benefits of state investment in development.

A long-term investment

Building a new community requires significant up-front investment. Expensive infrastructure, like roads and sewers, has to be installed long before any income from tax increases is received. The new town development corporations were funded by 60-year fixed-rate loans from the Treasury, supplemented by finance from other public bodies (such as the Highways Agency) and by the per capita funds from existing public-sector programmes to pay for things like schools, hospitals and some infrastructure. Later new towns were also able to borrow from the private sector, but the programme ended before this power was ever used.[17]

The importance of cheap land

The early new towns were able to buy land at agricultural prices (using compulsory-purchase powers where necessary), meaning that the increase in value that resulted from the development process was retained, initially, by their development corporations. After 1962, legislation was introduced that meant that some 'hope value' (ie the value that might be created by the 'hope' of future development) also had to be considered when compensation payments were calculated. This had a considerable impact on the income of the later corporations.

The financial performance of the new towns programme

Due to this ability to buy cheap land, and because of low interest rates at the time, the first new towns, such as Harlow, were so financially successful that some became net lenders to other public bodies. However, the cost of borrowing was a major financial burden for the Mark Three new towns in the 1970s and 1980s, owing to national inflation of interest rates and the forced sale of development corporation commercial assets from 1981 onwards, which removed income growth from this source. This limited the ability of these new towns to reinvest in their own renewal and upkeep.

The £4.75bn loan made to the new town development corporations by the Treasury was repaid in early 1999 (assisted by the sale of sites). Subsequently, by 2002, land-sale receipts had generated around £600m, of which £120m was reinvested in the new towns.[18] Research published by the TCPA in 2015 found that the government (via the Homes and Communities Agency) still owns a great deal of land in the new towns and continues to receive income from it.

The development corporations were able to sell freeholds and acquire land as the new towns grew. The corporations acted as housing associations, and housing built for rent was subsidised by the government in the same way that it would be for local authorities. As 'arms' of government, the housing policies for the new towns evolved alongside changing government policy. The new towns built up huge housing revenue accounts, which eventually had to be written off by the government. In later years, after the Housing Act 1980, revenue was raised by selling housing for owner-occupation through the 'Right to Buy' legislation, by selling housing land for sale or self-build, and by disposing of land to housing associations in order to deliver housing for rent or shared ownership.

The End of the New Towns Programme

In 1952, the incoming Conservative Government passed the Town Development Act, which provided financial support for housing and a range of infrastructure in 'Expanded Towns'. These were smaller, usually county, towns in need of regeneration, and the act enabled larger city authorities to make deals with these towns to accommodate some of their housing needs. The act had been introduced as a bill by the outgoing Labour Government, to supplement the new towns programme, but is considered by some historians as being retained by the Conservatives to replace the programme – as from that point onwards, the new towns began to lose favour.[19]

Political concern about the new towns began to increase in the 1960s. Both Labour and Conservative politicians criticised them for draining the cities of their young people and diverting funds away from the inner cities (in fact, only 17% of new town residents had come from London, and the funds for the new towns were loans being repaid with interest).[20] At this time, the earliest new towns were reaching a point at which their development corporations were not considered necessary – and so, the first few corporations were wound up, with the assets passing to a new body called the Commission for New Towns (created to ensure that the Treasury could retain what were then valuable assets).

The Commission for New Towns became the landlord for the land and property – including dwellings, a large proportion of which were social housing. Most of this property (shops, houses and industrial premises) produced rent, which the commission transferred in annual payments to the Treasury. Responsibilities for planning and roads were devolved to the relevant local authorities.

By the 1970s, the government had turned its attention to the inner cities, which were rapidly losing people and jobs due to de-industrialisation. In 1978, the Inner Urban Areas Act was passed; it transferred funds from the new and expanded towns programmes to inner-city regeneration schemes. This impacted on the resources for the designated new towns, which continued to develop but at a much slower pace. Forward-thinking corporations, such as that at Milton Keynes, were already anticipating the political changes and moving towards a more private-sector-driven development model.

Fig 3.22
New towns like Milton Keynes were still under construction when the development corporations were prematurely wound up.

'Here comes Maggie'

By the early 1980s, a wave of rioting in areas such as Brixton, South London, and Toxteth, Liverpool, forced the Conservatives to take action. Margaret Thatcher's government introduced enterprise zones and urban development corporations, which retained an emphasis on regenerating inner urban areas.

In this context of a focus on the regeneration of existing cities, the government ordered the winding up of the remaining development corporations and instructed the Commission for New Towns to dispose of its existing land and property portfolio. With few exceptions, these were sold on the open market. This action was to have a devastating impact on the new towns, many of which were still in their infancy (Fig 3.22). Land and property were far from reaching their potential value, and so the taxpayer was effectively robbed of a valuable income source. Social housing was sold to tenants or transferred to the local authority or housing associations.

Fig 3.23
Many iconic estates, such as James Stirling's Southgate estate in Runcorn (pictured here), were later wholly or partially demolished following problems with anti-social behaviour or the use of poor-quality materials.

Settling the assets

By 1996, all the new town development corporations had been wound up, and their assets passed to the local authority or sold to the private sector. Local authorities received a mixture of income-generating assets (such as the social housing, where residents had chosen the authority rather than a housing association) and community-related assets (everything from green spaces to community centres). Many of the income-generating assets later became liabilities, and local authorities did not have the funds to pay for the maintenance of things like social housing. In addition, the land transferred to authorities was subject to 'claw-back', whereby any increase in value of the land when it was used or sold by the authorities had to be passed to the Commission for New Towns or its successor body. Today, the Homes and Communities Agency still owns 4,303 hectares of land in the new towns (not all of this is former development corporation land). While the land still has claw-back covenants, the agency is working with authorities in partnership.

In Milton Keynes and Peterborough, forward-thinking development corporations created charitable trusts to take on the management of green spaces (eg The Parks Trust in Milton Keynes, and the Nene Park Trust in Peterborough) or community assets (MK Community Foundation). These organisations were endowed with land and property portfolios from which they have been able to generate income to reinvest in their new towns today, reflecting more than a glint of Howard's vision for long-term stewardship of community assets.

We will never know what might have been possible if the new towns programme had not been curtailed. As the 32 places designated under the programme continue to grow (and in places, decline), what is clear is that the programme provided a scale of ambition for improving the lives of millions of people that has not been rivalled since.

Lessons from the New Towns

Howard's garden city experiments suffered from the fiscal wariness of the company directors on the one hand and from the government's desire to control development on the other. The new towns were effectively an evolution of the garden city model but upscaled in geographic and population size as well as strategic economic purpose, and with a vastly different model of delivery.

In 2016, Stevenage will celebrate its 70th anniversary, and even the most recent designation is now 45 years old. Many of the new towns would no longer call themselves 'new'. The UK's 32 new towns today provide homes for 2.8 million people in 1.2m homes, amounting to 5.5% of the UK's total social-housing stock.[21] While their statistics on health and deprivation today are broadly in line with UK averages, the new towns also include pockets of some of the most deprived communities in the UK. The positive and negative legacies of the Development Corporations continue to inform the development of the new towns today.[23] So what are the key lessons that we can take away from the new towns?

Six key themes flow from this learning (Box 3.01):

Box 3.01: Key themes for learning from the new towns

1. Location and planning consent

2. Finance and investment

3. Ensure, and protect, delivery

4. Adopt strong, clear design and masterplanning

5. Plan for long-term stewardship

6. Ensure public support and engagement

Location and planning consent

Perhaps the most surprising lesson from the new towns programme is that finding sites for the developments was a local authority led process, with central government acting as *enabler*. There is a common misconception that the new towns were imposed by Westminster on places that did not want them. The new town sites of Milton Keynes and Warrington – two of the fastest-growing towns and cities in the UK – were promoted by the relevant county councils; likewise for Cwmbran, albeit at the invitation of the Welsh Ministry. For Cumbernauld and Craigavon, regional bodies were responsible for identifying needs and locations. While the minister ultimately designated each new town, and was often the one to suggest the use of the legislation, the need for a new community had usually been established by local authorities, politicians or experts in the preceding years. Indeed, the minister was often important in providing a 'voice' that was independent of local politics. He used the New Towns Act to help create a more balanced approach to development that included the social and economic investment made possible under the act. The dedicated consent regime provided by the New Towns Act meant that their corporations could quickly get on with the job.

Finance and investment

An important lesson from the new towns programme is that building new communities can be profitable for government. Since the £4.75bn-worth of loans taken out by their development corporations were paid back (with interest) in 1999, the land in the former new towns has continued to generate income for the Treasury. It is difficult to obtain a precise figure for the economic return of the new towns programme as some debt was written off by the government, but there has also been a huge increase in the value of their remaining assets. The new towns represented a significant up-front investment for the Treasury, but, overall, the investment has been returned, with interest – even without considering the non-monetary benefits to society.

Delivery

The new towns programme showed that the correct partnerships, with the necessary powers and resources, can deliver quickly and effectively. The new town development corporations were highly effective at delivering at speed because they had the autonomy to conduct the deals necessary to get 'spades in the ground'. They also had huge resources – and the best talent available – to make this happen.

The forced, premature winding up of the corporations (who had to sell their assets before they had reached maturity, and therefore their full value) also emphasises the need to have delivery bodies with a long enough life to do the job.

Design and masterplanning

One of the more direct legacies from garden city to new town was the role of a strong design vision. For places like Milton Keynes and Warrington, the masterplan set out by the corporations provided a framework upon which the towns were able to flourish. One of the clearest aspects of these frameworks was the concept of walkable neighbourhoods set within a framework of comprehensive green infrastructure. Originally introduced by the garden city pioneers, this feature was retained and expanded in the new town plans – and has since become embedded in general urban-design good practice.

Long-term stewardship

Perhaps the most important lesson of the new towns programme is that provision for the long-term stewardship of assets – at winding up of the corporation, but also in perpetuity – must be envisaged at an early stage, and ideally legally strengthened. The new town experience highlighted what can happen if this requirement is not enshrined in law. The land and income-generating assets of the new towns could have been used to pay for the long-term maintenance and management of the fantastic community facilities provided by the corporations. Instead, today many of the new towns look run down as councils lack the money for the upkeep of large areas of green space and community facilities. Those places where some form of stewardship body has been established demonstrate the scale of the missed opportunity. While long-term investment in community development was undoubtedly a strength of the new towns programme, its lack of a matching strategy for the long-term stewardship of community assets is undoubtedly one of its major failures – and a lesson to take forward when considering any new development, particularly in a time of austerity.

Public support and engagement

Compared with today's requirements for public engagement in the development process, opportunities in the era of the new towns were limited. Additionally, the earliest examples compromised public engagement for the sake of speed of delivery (due to government pressure). Later new towns, notably Milton Keynes, learnt this lesson and invested specific resources in monitoring the needs and views of incoming residents. The emphasis that the later development corporations put on community engagement is one of the key positive legacies in the new towns today. Many new towns exhibit a sense of civic pride – often represented in active community groups, which some residents identify as a legacy of the corporation's efforts.[22] Many people recognise that new towns are good places to bring up a family. Places like Cumbernauld have received critical awards as a result of their design. However, the positive experience of many new town residents is sometimes marred by the stigma attached to some of the less successful new towns, which have suffered from social deprivation and now look run down. One such example is Craigavon, where great efforts have been made to overcome some local stigma.

After the New Towns

The new towns programme was a seminal part of Britain's urbanism story. But when it ended (the last new town was designated in 1970, and the programme was wound up from the 1980s onwards as the government turned its attention to the inner cities), the need to house the nation did not disappear. A succession of governments would revisit the role of comprehensively planned new developments as a means to tackle the nation's continuing housing crisis. ◆

FROM NEW TOWNS
TO ECO-TOWNS

Successive governments have sought to address housing needs and returned periodically to the conclusion that large-scale, planned settlements are an important part of the solution. But as fashions and politics have changed, so have the approaches to delivery and even the terminology surrounding new communities (though never departing far from a set of powerful terms – 'garden city', 'new town' or, more recently, 'eco-town'). Periodically, the private sector, attracted by the prospect of significant returns, has made several attempts to deliver new communities without strong policy support from the government. In recent decades, we have come closer to achieving a contemporary programme of new communities, but it seems that politics and our development model – based on short-term financial returns to the private sector – have stood in the way of achieving the socially just and self-financing new communities envisaged by Howard and the garden city pioneers. While the previous chapter set out the evolution of the postwar new towns programme from the 1940s until the turn of the century, this chapter looks at the experience of other attempts at bringing forward large-scale new communities, from the 1960s until the present day.

Private-sector
New Towns

Although the private sector had played a huge role in delivering large-scale development between the wars, and much of the housing in the later new towns, the government rejected the idea of allowing it to play any significant role (as lead developers) in the new town development corporations themselves. The 1945 Reith Committee was clear that, unlike the publicly led corporations, the private sector could not be expected to behave in the interests of the public. However, the committee did recognise that, learning from the private

development companies at Letchworth and Welwyn, it would be possible for a non-governmental 'authorised association' to build a new town – although this option was not enshrined in the 1946 New Towns Act. In England, New Ash Green, South Woodham Ferrers and Cramlington, and the activities of Consortium Developments Ltd, are notable examples among several attempts by the private sector – alone or in partnership with local authorities – to make a small 'new town'.[1]

New Ash Green, Kent

In 1966, SPAN – a property-development company formed in the late 1950s, led by the architect and developer Geoffrey Townsend – received permission for the development

of 2,000 homes at New Ash Green. The scheme was designed by the architect Eric Lyons as a Modernist paradise, which was to include 450 homes for Greater London Council tenants in a 'Village planned as a "whole" place created for Twentieth Century living and providing for Twentieth Century people's needs' (Fig 4.01).[2] Just a few years later, the GLC were forced to pull out of the project for financial reasons. This was the start of a series of problems for SPAN, which was eventually forced to sell the project to Bovis Homes in 1971 for £3m. The development was criticised for attracting a narrow demographic but was an interesting attempt, which included a two-tiered management model that went some way towards Howard's vision of long-term stewardship.[3]

Fig 4.01
New Ash Green was a notable attempt at a private sector new community.

Cramlington New Town – a community prepared to invest in property. At present, 20,000 people live there. In the long term, it will be 80,000. Buying many different styles of houses to live in. At prices newcomers can afford. Alternatively, there are Housing Association and local authority houses and flats to rent with homes immediately available for key workers moving in with new industry.

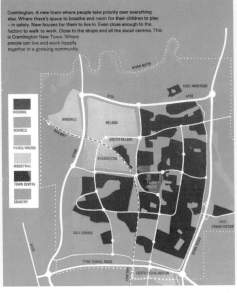

Cramlington. A new town where people take priority over everything else. Where there's space to breathe and room for their children to play – in safety. New houses for them to live in. Even close enough to the factory to walk to work. Close to the shops and all the social centres. This is Cramlington New Town. Where people can live and work happily together in a growing community.

Fig 4.02a/4.02b
Cramlington was an ambitious attempt to build a large-scale new community without invoking the New Towns Act.

Cramlington, Northumberland

In 1958, a group of local authorities and private housebuilders came together to plan a new community at a former mining village near Newcastle upon Tyne. Draft plans for an 'enterprise new town' of 40,000 people were approved by Northumberland County Council in 1961, and by the minister of housing and local government in 1963, at which time the predicted population rose to 48,000. Built by local construction companies, which grew to be Bellway Homes and Persimmon Homes, Cramlington has a current population of around 28,000.[4] By 1968, there had been discussions about using the New Towns Act or Town Development Act to accelerate delivery and ensure that the community facilities were in place to allow for the intended levels of commercial development (Fig 4.02). Cramlington was a focus of industrial development in the north-east at a time when traditional industries were in rapid decline.[5] In 1968, the council staff working on the project numbered just 12 – in stark contrast to staff levels in development corporations at the time, which could be up to 250. Cramlington remains a focus for commercial investment in the north-east,[6] and is Britain's largest new town built without a development corporation.

Fig 4.03
At South Woodham Ferrers, the private sector delivered within a strong local authority planning framework.

South Woodham Ferrers, Essex

In the 1970s, Essex County Council acquired land to develop a new community of 17,500 people in 4,600 homes at South Woodham Ferrers. The project was delivered mainly by the private sector, but within a tight planning and design framework set by the local authority (Fig 4.03). The council had adopted the recent *Essex Design Guide for Residential Areas* in response to concerns about the poor standards of speculative development in the county. The application of the guide to the development was, at the time, a pioneering approach – and instrumental in achieving a coherent yet distinct identity for the town.[7] The leadership and strategic planning role of the county council – including its land ownership – was fundamental to delivering the key up-front infrastructure needed for the development. Today its town centre is in need of regeneration, and design critics might highlight issues such as a

lack of permeability and too little 'green infrastructure' (with transport planning in the town having been a product of its time – ie car dominated). However, councils and delivery partners today can still learn from South Woodham Ferrers' approach to delivery, and the pioneering spirit of its design solutions.

Consortium Developments Ltd

Perhaps the most significant attempt at a truly private-sector-led new town was made in the 1980s by a group of volume housebuilders calling themselves 'Consortium Developments'. The group proposed a number of new communities – of 25,000 homes or more – to be delivered through private enterprise. However, none of these came to fruition as they were not promoted through the planning system and provoked bitter local opposition.[8]

Fig 4.04
Greentown was a collective action project established in the 1980s to build a 'cooperatively run and ecologically sound village community' in Milton Keynes.

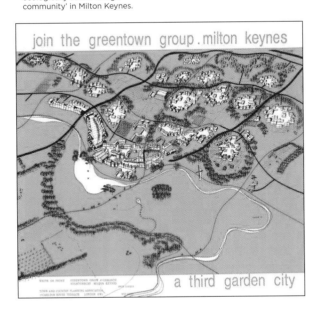

'Do-it-yourself' New Towns

There were also several attempts at 'Do-it-yourself new towns' by forward-thinking organisations – notably, the Greentown Group at Milton Keynes (Fig 4.04), the TCPA at Lightmoor, Telford (Fig 4.05) and Findhorn Eco Village in Moray, Scotland. In these cases, groups of individuals driven by the collective aim of a fairer and more cooperative way of living attempted to gain control of land and start their own communities. A combination of market forces (rising land values) and fearful local authorities prevented many of these schemes from becoming a reality.[9]

Fig 4.05
In 1980, the TCPA worked with Telford Development Corporation in an attempt to build Britain's third garden city at Lightmoor. The project has just celebrated its 30th birthday.

Between 1979 and 1997, the Conservative Government continued to focus on the privatisation of services and the deindustrialisation of Britain's cities. Urban policy focused on regeneration of the inner cities; new communities, particularly those led by the public sector, would remain out of favour. It would take a change of government for the consideration of new communities to take hold again.

Towards Sustainable Communities

Under Tony Blair's premiership, the government saw house prices rise and affordability start to pinch in London and the south-east alongside challenges of regeneration and renewal in many of Britain's post-industrial towns and cities, which continued to see their populations decline. The New Labour Government were renowned for setting housebuilding targets – with headline figures of 2m new homes by 2016, and 3m by 2020 – based upon a projected need of 240,000 new homes a year.

Through a regional approach to planning, new communities continued to be part of the housing mix in a succession of regional planning guidance documents and, later, regional spatial strategies. This process provided the evidence base for several of the new communities that today – 15 years later – are progressing through the planning system and have received support from subsequent government programmes. For example, the regional planning guidance for East Anglia[10] identified the need for new communities beyond the green belt in order to accommodate a rapidly growing Cambridge subregion. This led to the development of Cambourne, Longstanton-Oakington and, later, Northstowe – and, more recently, Alconbury Weald and Waterbeach.[11]

The Sustainable Communities Plan

This strategic consideration of housing need received a financial boost in 2003 with the Sustainable Communities Plan. The plan identified four south-east growth areas – Thames Gateway, Milton Keynes South Midlands, Ashford and the London–Stansted–Cambridge corridor – to be carried forward through the regional-strategy process, to accommodate large amounts of housing and related development, including employment, with a view to increasing housing supply in the south-east by 200,000 homes (Fig 4.06). The growth areas programme proposed through the Sustainable Communities Plan was perhaps the first time since the new towns that the concept of a planned new community had been considered in a holistic way, highlighting the importance of infrastructure, social and community development, good design and the reuse of public land. The programme forced all government departments to the table through the process, and helped to convince the Treasury that large-scale development could work even alongside the regeneration of other towns and cities.[12]

Though the growth areas programme led to some important infrastructure investments, it was less successful at engaging with local plan processes and with local opposition to specific developments; it was perceived by some as too 'top-down'.

The growth points programme

By 2005, within the context of a growing housing-affordability crisis and following the economist Kate Barker's two reviews of housing supply and land-use planning,[13] there was a desire to take further action to stimulate local growth. In 2006, the government established the growth points programme, in which local planning authorities took the lead. Councils were invited to propose additional housing

Fig 4.06
Locations of the growth areas and growth points in the south-east of England.

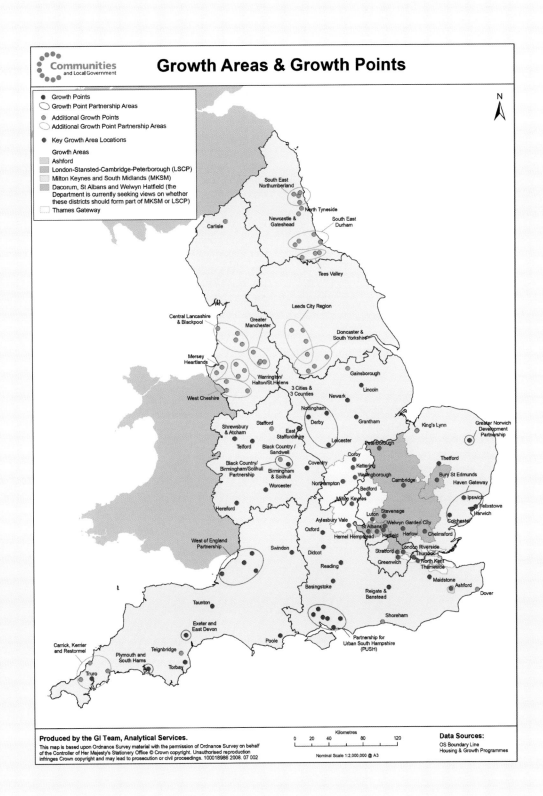

(minimum 20%) beyond existing plans as part of a wider growth strategy, in exchange for government help on infrastructure (particularly transport) and a modest grant to prepare infrastructure and community facilities. In the first phase of the programme, 29 growth points involving 70 local authorities produced plans for 100,000 extra homes in 45 towns and cities. The following year, the government extended the programme – and, for the first time, opened it up to councils in the north of England, with the ambition of delivering an additional 50,000 homes. The growth point initiative is regarded by the former Department for Communities and Local Government (DCLG) eco-towns policy leader, Henry Cleary, as perhaps the 'unsung hero' of the story.[14]

By 2007, 1.6m homes had been identified in existing Regional Spatial Strategies (RSS) and the 2003 Sustainable Communities Plan laid the foundation for around 650,000 homes in the four growth areas, according to a government white paper.[15] But this was not enough, and in a bid to reach a higher target of 240,000 new homes per year by 2016 and reduce carbon dioxide emissions by 80% below 1990 levels by 2050, the government launched the eco-towns programme.

Eco-towns

In 2007, as the international recession caused by the banking collapse hit, the government invited bids for 10 new communities with around 25,000 population each. The programme was accompanied by a Planning Policy Statement (PPS) that set out the high objectives to be met.

Eco-town standards

The eco-towns (Fig 4.07) were intended to be exemplars of good practice in new development, meeting the highest standards in terms of sustainable development and minimising carbon

Fig 4.07
Locations of the eco towns.

footprints, and achieving social justice and inclusive communities. The PPS[16] provided a range of minimum standards that were more challenging than would normally be required for new development. The standards set out in the PPS (Box 4.01) included requirements on everything from energy and flood risk to transport and governance. The eco-towns were to meet zero-carbon and lifetime homes standards; 40% of their total area was to be multifunctional and well-managed green space (at least half of which would be public open space), providing a net gain in local biodiversity. These eco-town criteria remain the most ambitious set of government-defined development standards ever seen in English policy-making. They are also the closest standards to the garden city principles ever set out in national policy. Developments such as North West Bicester, which received support under the eco-towns programme, are today being delivered with high standards of energy-efficient design and community development. At a time when the Conservative Government is committed to the removal of national design benchmarks and moving towards locally determined standards, which are often argued by developers to be 'unviable', the delivery of the eco-town standards – or something close to them – at places like Bicester demonstrate how a public commitment to national development standards is likely to lead to better development outcomes in the long run.

Box 4.01: Eco-town standards

▸ Zero-carbon over the course of a year (excluding transport emissions)

▸ A minimum of 30% affordable housing in each eco-town

▸ Each eco-town was to consist of 40% green space

▸ 'Higher' recycling rates, and making use of waste in new ways

▸ Homes must reach Code for Sustainable Homes level 4 or higher (level 6 was the highest available under CfSH)

▸ At least one job opportunity per house, which must be accessible by public transport, walking or cycling

▸ A range of services to suit a town of up to 20,000 homes, including shops and a primary school within easy walking distance of every home

▸ Real-time public-transport information in each home, and a public-transport link within 10 minutes' walk of every home

▸ A mixture of housing types and densities, and residents must have a say in how their town is run – via governance and in new and innovative ways.

▸ Community facilities must be in place before construction.[17]

A missed opportunity

The programme proved challenging because the government overlooked two fundamental issues: the need for local support and a strong policy context. Though the prospectus indicated that money would be made available to facilitate reviews of Regional Spatial Strategies in order to identify the broad locations of eco-towns,[18] this was not a requirement. Bids came forward without reference to a broader policy framework, despite the fact that the same government was still trying progress the Sustainable Communities Plan. Bids were invited without a requirement for prior public engagement, and within a timescale that led to many existing projects being dusted off and rebranded – or worse,

Fig 4.09
Construction began on the first homes in Whitehill & Bordon in 2016.

Fig 4.08
The first residents have now moved into North West Bicester (now called 'Elmsbrook'), an eco-town which has now received support as a 'garden town'.

projects being promoted effectively from nowhere. Of course, this approach led to public and local-authority resistance in nearly all locations. The exceptions were Bicester (where the bid was actually a local-authority proposal for a suburb to counter an eco-town proposed further west across the M40 motorway) (Fig 4.08), Whitehill & Bordon (a former army camp owned by the Ministry of Defence) (Fig 4.09) and the St Austell and China Clay Eco-communities (where there was no commercial promoter) – all of which were all given 'eco-town' status. By 2009, when the government published the eco-towns PPS, only these three sites and a fourth at Rackheath in Norfolk were at a sufficient stage to be included in the PPS, and the then-minister, John Healey, announced that further funding would be provided to support six more local authorities in developing proposals through regional and local plans in a bid to reach the intended target of 10 proposals by 2020.[19] Northstowe in Cambridgeshire was one of the developments classified as an eco-town in this second wave of the programme.

The New Communities Group

In 2009 – perhaps taking its cue from the 'New Towns Group', which provided shared learning for the new towns local authorities during that particular programme – the TCPA and the DCLG set up the 'Eco Development Group'. This comprised the local authorities bringing forward the eco-town developments (which are still going forward today, albeit under different titles), and members of the Homes and Communities Agency's large-scale development team (the Advisory Team for Large Applications). The group was designed to collectively help to develop the eco-towns proposals and share learning. This shared learning was valued by those involved, and when the programme was wound up following a change of government in 2010, the TCPA took on the management of the group (which is now self-financing). Reflecting the change in policy, the body rebranded in 2013 as the 'New Communities Group',[20] and at March 2017 includes 18 local authorities and one urban development corporation Ebbsfleet Development Corporation – all bringing forward large-scale development in

England, including those former eco-towns. The group provides political support and encourages a sharing of knowledge and best practice through seminars, workshops, study visits, parliamentary meetings and newsletters.

Back to the Future – From Eco-towns to Garden Cities

The year 2010 brought with it a new coalition government, who were quick to distance themselves from Labour's eco-towns programme. The public opposition to the schemes had made them too politically sensitive, and an easy target for criticism. They were also considered too top-down and therefore inconsistent with the secretary of state, Eric Pickles', localism agenda. This came alongside dramatic changes to the planning system as a whole – not least, the scrapping of Regional Spatial Strategies. The new government announced that the eco-towns PPS would be revoked as part of a streamlining of planning guidance, though policies for North West Bicester were to be saved until a local plan could be put in place.[21] It would take three years and a series of strategic environmental assessments before the document was revoked, in 2015. Meanwhile, those places that had received support through the scheme continued to drive their developments forward – retaining, for the most part, their commitment to the standards set out in the PPS. As we explore in Chapter 5, while the change in government in 2010 signalled a move away from eco-towns it heralded the start of a renewed interest in the garden city movement. ◆

chapter 5

TODAY'S CHALLENGES

Over a century after the Garden City movement began, the nation is still dealing with inadequate housing and huge social inequalities. Before exploring, in Chapter 6, the role of new garden cities in addressing these issues, this chapter looks at the roots of some of the contemporary challenges in Britain: the housing crisis, public health and climate change. While Chapter 3 outlined how new towns, and new communities more generally, have fallen in and out of favour over the past 70 years, this chapter looks at some of the social, economic and environmental drivers during the same period, setting the scene for how new garden cities can be part of the solution.

The Housing Crisis

The nature of the UK's housing crisis is both complex and severe. Parts of the country face a chronic undersupply of homes: we have failed to build enough new dwellings to meet demand for decades (Figs 5.01 and 5.02). In other parts of the country, the challenge is regeneration of our existing communities and the quality of existing social housing. Britain's housing crisis has been building for a generation, but it wasn't always this way. Following the second world war, where there was a strong alignment of positive planning and public investment, we regularly delivered over 300,000 public- and private-sector homes annually. As highlighted in Chapter 3, between the 1940s and 1960s we built 32 new towns UK-wide, which still house over 2.8 million people. But this is not simply a question of numbers. There is a growing concern that place-making and quality are being sacrificed for speed, and an awareness that even when the planning system does give consents the private sector is reluctant to build at the necessary rate.

A founding garden city principle was providing mixed-tenure homes and housing types that were genuinely affordable. Letchworth and Welwyn both included co-partnership housing models that provided a unique form of tenure, combining features

Fig 5.01/5.02
England's housing crisis
has been building for a
generation and highlights
stark inequalities across
the nation.

House building in England since 1923

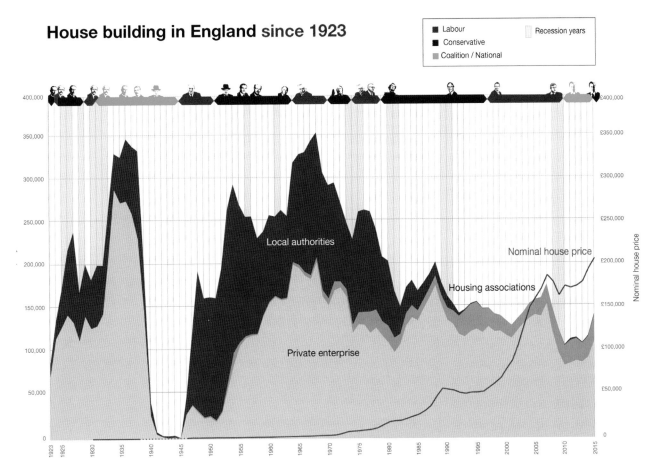

Legend:
- ■ Labour
- ■ Conservative
- ■ Coalition / National
- ▨ Recession years

Local authorities

Housing associations

Nominal house price

Private enterprise

Sources: DCLG, Shelter analysis
Images (1946-2015): A Right To Build, Architecture 00:/, 2012http://issuu.com/architecture00/docs/arighttobuild

Fig 5.03
The dramatic shift in housing delivery since the post-second-world-war period.

of a tenant cooperative with a limited-dividend company. Just under a third of all the homes in Letchworth Garden City (31%) remain socially rented today,[1] which is part of the town's success.

As explored in Chapter 3, the postwar new towns also had a strong social-housing focus. For example, between 69 and 97% of housing in the Mark One new towns were for social rent.[2, 3] Today, the role of the public sector in delivering social and affordable housing is unrecognisable from that of the postwar period (Fig 5.03). In 2014-15, councils built only 2,520 homes across the UK – and of these, just 1,360 were in England.[4]

Housing associations have helped fill this gap; however, this is only a fraction of what the public sector built previously. The dominant model of providing new homes is now private-sector delivery. The private sector is building at roughly its postwar average rate and may be able to increase output, but only marginally; as a consequence, we are only realising around half the homes needed. With over 1.2 million people on council-housing waiting lists,[5] and more than 81,000 households homeless in England in 2013/14,[6] it is increasingly clear that the market alone will not deliver the homes that the nation needs.

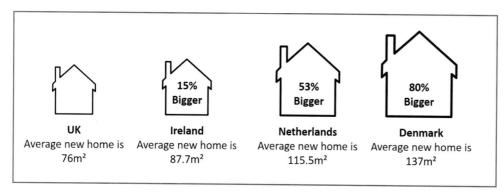

UK
Average new home is 76m²

15% Bigger

Ireland
Average new home is 87.7m²

53% Bigger

Netherlands
Average new home is 115.5m²

80% Bigger

Denmark
Average new home is 137m²

Fig 5.04
Britain is building some of the smallest homes in Europe.

In 2015-16 168,350 new homes were completed across the whole of the UK[7] – of which 139,840 were in England.[8] Set against this is the projected formation of at least 220,000 new households each year in England until 2031.[9] With demand for new homes vastly outstripping supply, there is increasing pressure on house prices and rents. These figures also fail to take account of the backlog built up during years of undersupply. To address the shortfall that has occurred since 2011, England would need to build an average of 312,000 homes a year between 2016 and 2020. This is more than 50% higher than the current government's target of 1,000,000 new homes – itself seen by most commentators as unachievable.

The housing crisis is most severe in London, the south-east and the east of England, where 55% of the dwellings required nationally need to be located. Even if these homes were actually built, projections as of 2016 suggest that couples aged 25–35 will still be less able to own a home in 2031 than their counterparts were in 2011.

Housing is not just a numbers game; what about quality?

The garden city ideals not only set out the need for mixed-tenure homes and housing types. They also call for those homes to be beautifully and imaginatively designed, with gardens, combining the best of town and country. Similarly, the postwar new towns

were at the forefront of the drive for decent space standards in new homes.

Today, not only are we failing to build enough dwellings but the ones we are building are often of poor quality. According to the Royal Institute of British Architects (RIBA), we are constructing the smallest homes in western Europe (Fig 5.04) and over 50% of the new homes being built today are too small for families.[10] This wasn't always the case.

The Parker Morris space standards

The 'Parker Morris' space standards were named after Sir Parker Morris, who chaired a 1961 subcommittee of the Central Housing Advisory Committee that produced a report called 'Homes for today and tomorrow'.[11] It stated: 'Additional space is an important long-term investment, for if a house or flat is large enough it can usually be brought up-to-date as it gets older, but if there is not enough space improvements can be impossible, or at least unduly expensive.' Following the report's publication, many local authorities adopted the Parker Morris space standards; they become mandatory for all housing built in new towns from 1967, and all council housing from 1969.[12]

While the Parker Morris standards certainly had an impact on the quality of new housing, particularly in the new towns, some felt that they were neither generous enough nor applied widely enough. This led to the government's then regeneration agency, English Partnerships (now known as the Homes and Communities Agency), to require space standards of 'Parker Morris plus 10%' for developments on its own land from 2008.[13] In 2010, the Greater London Authority followed suit, setting out space standards in the *London Housing Design Guide*. The guide states:

In recent years London has been providing some of the smallest homes in the developed world and too many developments of a low quality. This is not something to be proud of and is not sustainable. The new London standards and guidance are intended to encourage provision of enough space in dwellings to ensure homes can be flexibly used by a range of residents. They also aim to ensure that space can be sensibly allocated to different functions, with adequate room sizes and storage integrated into the planning.[14]

Towards locally prescribed standards

However, both the Coalition Government (since 2010) and the Conservative Government (since May 2015) have favoured a move away from setting nationally prescribed standards. In March 2015, the Coalition published new national technical standards for housing in England. This system replaced the Code for Sustainable Homes, with new, additional 'optional' building standards on water and access and a nationally described space standard (referred to as 'the new national technical standards').[15]

Research by the RIBA into these standards has found that 'local authorities will struggle to set the new space standard as it is over complicated, costs too much and will take too long'.[16] In a report, '#HomeWise: Space Standards for Homes',[17] the RIBA found that 'more than half of the new homes being built today are not big enough to meet the needs of the people who buy them. This squeeze on the size of our houses is depriving thousands of families of the space needed for them to live comfortably.' The Housing White Paper, published in February 2017 suggests the existing nationally described space standards will be removed to increase flexibility, providing further challenges to securing homes that meet people's needs.

Public Health

The planning system, like the garden cities, has its roots in the public-health movement. Improved planning and better housing have long been identified as essential for improving the health of communities, reducing health inequalities and cutting costs for the taxpayer. The Building Research Establishment (BRE) has calculated that the annual cost of poor housing to the National Health Service (NHS) is at least £1.4bn.[18]

The garden city movement was strongly driven by the need to give people a better quality of life. In 1938, Norman Macfadyen wrote the following:

A Garden City is surrounded by an open belt of country. This is an important factor. It makes for health, it limits the size of the town, it provides small holdings, allotments, playing fields, and walks for those who want them, and binds the people of the town into a unity. This unity gives an added interest to life and provides for a healthy social life, not an irritating one, because the planning ensures that every family shall have its separate and distinct house and garden, but a life which tends to a higher standard. If this paper points to anything, it is that this better condition of living for all will react favourably on the health of the individual. In short, our Garden City conditions are the healthiest known in this country under present conditions.[19]

As Macfadyen's paper *Health and Garden Cities* highlights, having easy access to high-quality parks and gardens improves mental health and levels of physical activity (Fig 5.05). Although many of the diseases quoted in the paper are no longer as common in the UK today as they were almost 80 years ago, the country is plagued by new diseases such as obesity – rates of which have tripled since the 1980s.[20] Furthermore, people living in the most deprived parts of England often have less access to green space than in wealthier areas They also experience the worst air quality, and are more likely to suffer from cardiorespiratory diseases.

Planning for health

Despite being rooted in public health, planning is a discipline that, over recent decades, has had little formal contact with health. Different workplace cultures, professional languages and reporting regimes have helped to exacerbate this divide. However, the government is trying to bring about change, with widespread reforms to both the planning and health sectors – including a requirement on planners to work with public-health organisations, and a new public-health responsibility for councils.

From roughly 2010 to 2016, the government has sought to reunite planning and public health using two key sets of reforms. First, the national planning-policy framework

Fig 5.05
Good planning can facilitate healthy lifestyles by encouraging walking and cycling.

– the overarching guidance for local authorities when drawing up plans and assessing development proposals – requires planners to promote healthy communities, use evidence to assess health and wellbeing needs, and work with public-health leaders and organisations. Second, the Health and Social Care Act 2012 transferred the responsibility for public health to upper-tier (eg counties and unitary) local authorities from April 2013. It also required the creation of health and wellbeing boards, to bring together key commissioners from the local NHS and local government to strategically plan local health and social-care services.

These reforms strengthen the argument for recognising and valuing the influence that planning, housing and other environmental functions have on improving health and wellbeing, and in reducing health inequalities. However, they are set against significant cuts to local-authority public-health budgets. The Local Government Association (LGA) reports: 'Councils will receive £77m less from Government for public health in 2016/17 and £84m less in 2017/18. This is on top of a £200m in year cut in 2015/16.'[21] Councillor Izzi Seccombe, the LGA's community wellbeing spokesperson, highlights the problem faced by councils: 'Devolving public health to local government was a positive step, and councils have embraced these new responsibilities. However ... the significant cuts to public health grants will have a major impact on the many prevention and early intervention services carried out by councils. These include combating the nation's obesity problem'.[22]

Healthy new towns

Despite the cuts to public health budgets, in 2015 NHS England launched a 'Healthy New Towns' programme as part of their five-year vision, recognizing that 'there is a huge opportunity to shape places to radically improve population health, integrate health and care services, and offer new digital and virtual care fit for the future.'[23] NHS England invited expressions of interest from development sites of up to 10,000 homes, and received over 100 proposals. In 2016 NHS England announced support for 10 sites that will go forward as pilot programmes 10 sites that will go forward as pilot programmes, helping to demonstrate how a fresh approach to creating healthy new towns will:[24]

▸ Build new communities that support social cohesion, physical and mental wellbeing, walking cycling and sports in place of our current 'obesogenic' built environments.

▸ Maximise the impact of housing, including specialist housing, in improving health and wellbeing.

▸ Leapfrog old ways of providing community health and social care services by designing-in the use of new digital technologies to help people live independently in their own homes.

▸ Share land and buildings infrastructure such as new NHS clinics, schools, police and fire stations and other public services.[25]

Both the NHS England's Healthy New Towns programme and the fact that local authorities find themselves at the forefront of public health (despite the significant financial challenges that they face) provide an opportunity to reconnect planning and health to improve the wellbeing of both people and places. When it comes to planning new settlements, garden cities provide a blueprint for how to incorporate public-health planning from the start.

Although written over seven decades ago, Macfadyen's paper serves to demonstrate that the radical ideals of the garden city movement remain highly relevant in the 21st century, providing a crucial foundation for high-quality inclusive places and the creation of new jobs and truly sustainable, healthy lifestyles.

Climate Change

Climate change is the greatest long-term challenge facing human development. It is clearly our biggest economic and social challenge, because without climate stability we cannot forge a long-term, sustainable and fair society in the future. The science is clear, and examples from Europe, like Freiburg in Germany (Fig 5.06), and the rest of the world demonstrate that climate change can be tackled by shaping new and existing developments in ways that reduce carbon dioxide emissions and create resilience to extreme weather events such as flooding and heatwaves (Fig 5.07). However, as a nation we are not acting anywhere near fast enough.

The UN Paris climate agreement is clear that the global economy will need to be zero carbon by the second half of the 21st century; with its additional, distinct statement that this will take longer for developing economies, this implies much earlier zero carbon for developed countries like the UK. The UK Committee on Climate Change (CCC) also say, 'meeting the 2050 target will require that emissions from energy use – power, heat and transport – are almost eliminated.'[26]

While action in the 1990s and the 2000s (for example, the introduction of the world-leading Climate Change Act in 2008, alongside government initiatives like the eco-towns programme highlighted in Chapter 4, the Code for Sustainable Homes and the 2016 Zero Carbon Homes policy) set us on a positive pathway to tackling greenhouse-gas emissions in our homes and communities, much of this policy framework has subsequently been undone. While the Climate Change Act 2008 still remains on statute, with a target of 80% emissions reductions by 2050 compared to a 1990 baseline, the other policies mentioned above have all been scrapped by the government from 2010 onwards.

Fig 5.06
The UK has much to learn from places like Freiburg, where sustainable travel, green roofs, solar panels and community-led housing models combine to create low carbon neighbourhoods.

Fig 5.07
Flooding in Carlisle in 2016; it is no longer possible to ignore the impacts of climate change in Britain.

Delivering climate-change action is increasingly complex because of the fragmented planning system in Britain; severe opposition to some forms of renewable energy, such as onshore wind farms; and the prioritisation of economic growth over sustainable development by successive governments.

Our failure to act on climate change is short-sighted. We are missing a major opportunity to create a vibrant, sustainable low-carbon economy. We are also failing to ensure that our communities will be resilient in the face of climate change in the future.

While there is no longer a mandatory set of government sustainability standards for new homes and communities, the creation of new garden cities provides a significant opportunity to develop low-carbon solutions at scale – creating communities that are environmentally, socially and economically sound. After all, Howard's original vision addressed environmental, social and economic concerns – which today we would call the pillars of 'sustainable development' – with the aim of achieving environmental resilience.

A major advantage of creating a new garden city is that low- and zero-carbon solutions can be laid down across a whole town, so that individual buildings can be incorporated into combined solutions rather than each being developed in isolation.

Facing the Future

There is no doubt that the nation now faces a choice: continue to ignore the accelerating climate and housing crisis around us, or seize the opportunity to create a better future. Time is not on our side on either issue, which is why garden cities are much more than a historical curiosity. They are a key way of solving real problems that will define the 21st century. The following chapter brings together the lessons explored so far in this book, and explains how new garden cities are a vital part of the solutions needed to face these challenges head-on. ◆

chapter 6

WHY NEW GARDEN CITIES ARE PART OF THE SOLUTION

This chapter explores the political debate about the role of modern garden cities as part of a 'portfolio' of solutions to the problems described in Chapter 5. Ebenezer Howard could not know that many of the ideas he set out, such as the need for green infrastructure or rapid public transport, would also help to address more recent 21st-century problems such as climate change and obesity.

The chapter also sets out what the garden city model means today, and makes the case for creating highly sustainable new communities by addressing, head on, some of the key criticisms of this approach.

What's in a Name? The Battle of the Garden City 'Brand'

One of the challenges the Association has faced during the re-invigorated campaign for new garden cities is one faced by former colleagues in the 1930s, and that is the use (and abuse) of the term 'garden city'. Increasing political interest in new garden cities has brought with it a rush of people keen to brand their development as garden cities or suburbs, when often they are just 'leafy and green' and far from meet the principles of the movement. Of course, the association of the term 'garden city' with desirable, high-quality green and walkable neighbourhoods is in itself a big part of the attraction for politicians battling with people who are resisting new development after a generation of being subjected to poor quality housing. But it is a unique and precious concept that the TCPA has had to work hard to protect. As 'garden cities' has become a bit of a political buzz word, other terms such as 'garden towns', 'garden villages' and 'garden communities' have also emerged. These terms are being used to describe development which - to differing degrees - aspire to the cachet of the garden city brand but for one reason or another are considered by the promoters to be likely to fall short. This makes communicating the benefits of real garden cities to public and professionals alike even more challenging.

New garden cities represent an approach to contemporary development that aims to achieve the highest standards of resilient and inclusive place-making with tried-and-tested models of finance and delivery from over a century of learning about large-scale development. They are not about mimicking the look of the Arts and Crafts design of the original garden cities, but about combining the strong place-making objectives and participative democracy of the garden city movement with the fast and efficient delivery of the new towns programme, learning the lessons – good and bad – from what has been done before.

The TCPA has defined these characteristics as the 'garden city principles'. Part 2 of this book looks in detail at these principles and how to apply them to contemporary urban development, but for now it is enough to understand that a garden city is a holistically planned new settlement that enhances the natural environment and offers high-quality affordable housing and locally accessible work in beautiful, healthy and sociable communities. The garden city principles are an indivisible and interlocking framework for their delivery.

The Role of New Garden Cities in Contemporary Public Policy

Advocates of new garden cities state three powerful reasons why they are an important part of the solution to the nation's housing crisis. (Box 6.01):

Political Support for New Garden Cities

The recognition that a new generation of garden cities could form part of the solution to Britain's housing problems began in 2011 with the TCPA's publication of *Re-imagining Garden Cities for the 21st Century*, which brought together practical

Box 6.01: 'The case for new garden cities'

1. The scale of the housing crisis means that the current plot-by-plot approach is not sufficient to meet the nation's requirements. There needs to be a more coordinated and strategic approach to the delivery of homes through larger-scale developments.

2. Reducing carbon emissions and building-in climate resilience are best achieved through early planning and design; the holistic approach offered by the garden city movement enables genuine sustainable-development principles to be planned for and embedded in the development from the outset.

3. History has shown (eg through the new towns programme) that, properly managed and underwritten by the capture of land values, new communities can be an economically efficient way to achieve the growth we need.

lessons from the garden cities and new towns. Following initial support from the then housing minister, Grant Shapps, the subsequent three years saw significant political momentum on the issue. In January 2012, the prime minister and deputy prime minister announced their support for a new wave of English garden cites, promising a prospectus to support local authorities keen to bring forward proposals. Then, in March 2012, the National Planning Policy Framework was published, with broad support for garden city principles.[1] But with a lack of any detailed articulation of what this meant on the ground, it was left to organisations such as the TCPA to fill this gap by producing documents designed to make these ideas a reality (see Fig 6.01).[2]

Meanwhile, further interest in the garden city model was generated by the 2013 launch of the Wolfson Economics Prize,[3] which asked for responses to the question 'How would you deliver a new Garden City which is visionary, economically viable, and popular?', focusing on how a wholly private-sector-driven new-community model could be achieved. This signalled a renewed interest in private-sector investment in garden cities.

Fig 6.01
The TCPA's campaign for a new generation of garden cities has involved building cross-sector consensus, research and guidance on how to apply the garden city principles and how to update the New Towns Act to make a new programme a reality.

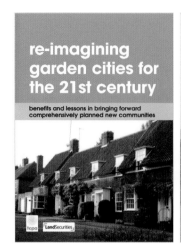

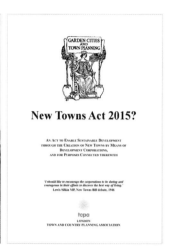

'Locally led' garden cities

By April 2014, two years after the prime minister first announced his support for a new wave of British garden cities, and following pressure from the Liberal Democrat side of the then Conservative–Lib Dem coalition,[4] the long-awaited 'locally led garden cities' prospectus was launched. It invited expressions of interest for proposals for new communities with 15,000 or more homes that demonstrated 'local support', 'scale', 'connectivity', 'robust delivery arrangements' and 'commercial viability' – and which favoured sites with a 'high proportion of brownfield land'.

Much of the supporting text of the prospectus said the right things about being ambitious, innovative and 'delivering inspirational new Garden Cities fit for the 21st Century'. When first mooted, the prospectus offered an opportunity for the government to drive forward a new programme of garden cities as an essential contribution to efforts to meet the annual need for over 220,000 new homes. While a competition of this nature was not considered an ideal approach by everyone, it had the potential to generate renewed interest in new garden cities if carefully handled and backed up with the appropriate policy and financial support.

However, with a lack of locational criteria or strategic approach, no requirement for expressions of interest to demonstrate how their projects would apply garden city principles, no new funding and lack of clarity on how the programme would work with existing planning processes, achieving the prospectus's ambitions has, to date, proved to be challenging. Aside from the prospectus approach, Local Plan processes provide an opportunity to bring forward new communities at a range of scales using garden city principles. However, without a strategic, 'larger than local' approach, it is unlikely that large-scale development will be delivered in the places where it is needed most.

Cross-party support for garden cities

Campaigns like that by the TCPA achieved a measure of cross-party support for garden cities in the run-up to the 2015 general election. The prime minister, deputy prime minister and the leader of the opposition Labour party all articulated their support for a new generation of garden cities, and they were mentioned in the three main parties' election manifestos. In January 2014, the then Labour leader, Ed Miliband, appointed Sir Michael Lyons to chair a housing commission, exploring evidence and opportunities for addressing the nation's housing needs. Among the many findings of the final report, *Mobilising across the nation to build the homes our children need*,[5] was the recommendation that the next government should immediately initiate a programme of garden cities and suburbs – to be delivered by new garden city development corporations and 'New Homes' corporations based on reformed new towns legislation.

Despite garden city principles gaining significant political support, however, none of the main Westminster parties has adequately addressed the question of how to deliver high-quality and comprehensively planned new communities, whose long gestation naturally transcends electoral cycles. This is, of course, because the matter involves addressing the difficult and politically sensitive issues of consent, land value (and compensation) and ensuring high standards of development within environmental limits.

Taking stock in Spring 2017

In 2015, a new Conservative government brought with a manifesto commitment to `support locally-led garden cities and towns, [ensuring] new homes are matched by the infrastructure to support them'.

Several projects had already received support under the initiative; however, in March 2016, a budget report announced support for the construction of a new wave of garden towns and cities, with potential for 100,000 homes.[6]

There were three main elements to this support.

Firstly capacity support, assisted by a new prospectus. Second, a commitment to update legislation to 'speed up and simplify the process … '. Third, to introduce 'incentives' for places willing to commit to housing over and above their assessed housing need. Further details

Fig 6.02
Elmsbrook, the first phase of 'North West Bicester'; in 2015, Cherwell Council received support for the development of the town through the 'garden towns' initiative.

were provided by the DCLG, including an offer of support for 'Garden Villages' of 1,500–10,000 homes (an idea which concerns TCPA in terms of scale and lack of requirement to commit to the jobs and facilities that were the cornerstone of the original garden villages), and as continued support for communities over 10,000 homes. Over 50 local authorities submitted bids for support.

By March 2017, a total of 24 projects have been supported through this policy (see Fig 8.05). Meanwhile progress on the welcome commitment to update the New Towns legislation, was disrupted by what followed in 2016: 'Brexit', a new Prime Minister, a new Housing and Planning Minister, and promise of a Housing White Paper. The TCPA published a joint statement with the Local Government Association and seven ambitious local authorities, setting out details how the White Paper must commit to updating the Act.

The Paper, 'Fixing our Broken Housing Market', arrived in February 2017, and with it a renewed commitment from government in support of a 'new generation of new communities'. At the time of writing, government has accepted an amendment to the Neighbourhood Planning Bill 2017 to make New Town Development Corporations more 'locally accountable'. This is a landmark change but only the start of changes needed to make the legislation fit for purpose today. Without also amending the legislation to provide for long-term stewardship and good place-making, we run the risk of failing to learn from the past and missing the opportunity to build the high quality, resilient and inclusive new communities the nation deserves. TCPA is working with the Department and time will tell if this government grasps the opportunity or ducks the wider changes for a future administration to deal with.[7]

Key Criticisms of the Garden City Approach

Though there has been significant political momentum on new garden cities, the model has its critics. Many key criticisms of the garden city approach have been debated for over a century; others tend to stem from a misunderstanding of what a new garden city is. This confusion isn't helped by a host of new terms such as 'garden villages', 'garden towns' and 'garden communities', some of which have little obvious connection to the original principles. This section attempts to unpick key criticisms of the garden city model.

'Garden cities detract from the need to invest in inner-city brownfield sites'

From the mid-1970s, successive governments have turned their attention to the growing inner-city question. Driven by civil unrest, there has been a desire to focus new development in existing urban areas rather than creating new ones. Initiatives such as the Urban Task Force of the 1990s and countryside-protection campaigns have argued that there is enough 'brownfield' – ie previously developed, often urban – land to meet the nation's housing needs.

This argument is partly about a desire to protect 'England's green and pleasant land', and partly about densifying development in order to achieve the 'critical mass' required for certain energy or transport networks. In fact, where we build the homes is not

a question of using either brownfield or greenfield land but one of choosing the most sustainable locations for new and renewed communities (as discussed in Chapter 8). For example, many brownfield sites have a much higher ecological value than agricultural land[8] – so blanket assumptions about where to build can lead to perverse outcomes.

Studies have shown that there are enough brownfield sites to accommodate up to 1.5m homes.[9] However, given that current population forecasts indicate over 220,000 new homes will be required each year up to 2031, then even if all these sites could be developed, they would provide land for only six years of supply. Furthermore, because only 54% of the homes required since 2011 have been built, we actually need to build over 310,000 homes a year to catch up by 2020. It is also unlikely that all these brownfield sites should or could be developed; some will be cherished by local communities for their current biodiversity and/or amenity value, and former industrial sites might be difficult and expensive to clean up or poorly served by public transport.

A second strand of this criticism concerns the green belt. There currently is a fierce debate about whether new garden cities should be built on green belt surrounding major conurbations like London or Cambridge. There is no easy answer to this question, but in principle the original notion of garden cities being built beyond green-belt boundaries and of limited size remains sound – particularly in the context of London, where the green belt fulfils other valuable functions. The notion of a network of highly sustainable 'sociable cities' offers a strategic solution to growth, but this does not mean that there aren't opportunities to rethink current green-belt boundaries in some places.

'New garden cities are anti-urban low-density, unsustainable urban sprawl that encourages car use'

A common misconception is that the garden city approach means low-density living. This is understandable given that Unwin's 'standard' of 12 dwellings to the acre (30 to the hectare) was applied at Letchworth and then, being included in the Tudor Walters Report in 1919,[10] became almost a universal norm for suburban development around London and other conurbations. This criticism is compounded by the fact that new towns were also characterised by low-to-medium-density living, thanks in part to low land prices as well as in reaction to the high-density slums that both models were intended to depart from.

However, Unwin actually believed in a variety of densities across developments.[11] There is no specified density for new garden cities, and a range across different areas is expected – eg there would be higher densities around transport hubs and neighbourhood centres. The test is the extent to which the density applied allows for the realisation of the garden city principles, which include creating walkable neighbourhoods and providing access to sustainable public transport. Density should allow for this provision, but it may be achieved in different ways in different places – for example by learning from countries like Germany, which shares spaces like community gardens where private gardens are not possible. Because new garden cities can deal with housing growth on larger, strategic sites, they can meet housing need over the long term in the most sustainable way.

'Garden cities will be soulless commuter towns'

Despite a fundamental principle of garden cities being that sufficient local jobs would be provided (see Chapter 1), both garden cities and new towns are often assumed to be soulless dormitory towns. To add to the confusion, Welwyn Garden City's proximity to London meant that quite quickly, and to the dismay of garden city supporters, it was marketed as a great place from which to commute to the capital.

In fact, more people travel to work each day within successful new communities such as Stevenage and Milton Keynes than commute to jobs elsewhere. The 2011 Census[12] revealed that in Stevenage there was a net inflow of over 2,000 workers the town (18,608 Stevenage residents commuted out for work, while 20,770 workers in-commuted). In Milton Keynes, the figures are even more impressive: the same census showed that there was net inward commuting to Milton Keynes of over 16,000 people. A study carried out by Milton Keynes Council in 2012[13] predicts that by 2026, net inward commuting will involve around 31,000 people.

'Garden cities will cost too much for any government to build'

Capturing the increased land values arising from the granting of planning permission distinguished the crucial, and highly, successful funding model used in the development of the original garden cities and the postwar new towns (see Chapter see Chapter 2 and Chapter 3). Today, the government can play a key role in laying the foundation for action by considering how land values can best be used for the long-term benefit of the community. Loans from the private or public sectors will also be necessary to fund up-front infrastructure, but history shows how profitable an enterprise building new communities can be. As well as these direct gains there are significant, wider benefits to the economy through, for example, construction expenditure.

'Garden cities divert investment away from existing towns and cities'

It is true that by the 1970s there was concern that new towns were drawing growth away from inner London. However, this was in era in which London's overall population was in decline. Circumstances are very different today: the nation's population has grown by 10 million since 1964, with roughly half of this growth occurring since 2001.[14]

No one is suggesting that garden cities are the only way of meeting our housing needs. In fact, we need a 'portfolio' approach of different solutions, recognising the varying needs of Britain's regions and localities. Regeneration remains a key priority, however, and the garden city principles can be applied to this task. England needs a proper urban policy, in which garden cities and regeneration are seen as complementary interventions.

'Garden cities look like something from *The Truman Show* – boring or ugly, or both'

New towns were designed to be exemplars of quality development, but today many look unappealing and run-down. However, this is largely because their financial assets were removed, leaving them without the necessary resources for upkeep and renewal. In delivering new garden cities, it is possible to avoid the mistakes of the past if we focus on the quality of new places – not just the number of houses – and, as discussed in Chapter 10, we ensure that they are endowed with sufficient assets to secure long-term income for future maintenance. Essentially, garden cities should be places of high-quality design and innovation – and applying their principals properly should ensure that these aims are realised.

'Garden cities are often imposed on communities'

Garden cities give people a real opportunity to shape the development and ongoing direction of their community once it has been established. However, there is no point in pretending that the process of agreeing where new examples should go will be easy. A new settlement can have local, regional and national significance in meeting housing needs, but its impacts are focused on those residents who live near the site. The formal planning process allows for democratic scrutiny and individuals' civil rights to be consulted, but a much wider and ambitious notion of active participation is necessary to bring people into decisions in a meaningful

way. In principle, it's much easier to have this debate about one large-scale development than about 100 speculative proposals, some of which may be approved against local or neighbourhood plan policy.

'Garden cities cannot deliver affordable homes'

Garden cities are defined by their focus on providing genuinely affordable homes for those on low and moderate incomes, so that ordinary people are not denied good housing and a decent quality of life. In fact, new garden cities led by powerful development corporations can provide diverse housing-tenure options, delivered by a range of providers – from private-sector housebuilders to partnerships with housing associations and smaller housing providers such as cooperatives and community land trusts. Self-/custom-build homes should be an important part of the housing mix in new garden cities, and the masterplanning approach can designate land for this purpose – preferably as serviced plots.

A third of the homes in Letchworth, the world's first garden city, are still social-rented.[15] Today's new garden cities should aim to be just as ambitious.

Towards a Shared Vision for Tomorrow

There is no 'silver-bullet' solution to addressing the chronic housing challenges facing the nation; we need a whole portfolio of solutions. This chapter has attempted to explain how 21st-century garden cities could be an essential part of that solution. New garden cities are simply models of planned urban development that apply good principles of place-making; progressive social and environmental values; and, importantly, a fair distribution of the profits of the development process. Combined, these principles can help us find a better way to live. ◆

PART 2

DELIVERING THE FUTURE

◆ *Part 1 of this book explored the background to the garden city movement. It traced a history back half a millennium to Thomas More's* Utopia *and fo rward through the new towns movement and beyond, highlighting some of the key lessons we have learned in over a century of delivering planned new communities. It also set out the background to today's challenges and the role of new garden cities in helping addressing them. Finally, it gave a flavour of the political debate surrounding the role of new communities and the challenges and opportunities that this presents.*

◆ *Part 2 focuses on how to make these ideas a reality. Chapter 7 provides an overview of the garden city principles and what they mean in the 21st century. Chapters 8–14 then provide a practical view of the standards necessary, and opportunities available, to achieve these principles in new developments today. Planning a new community is a complex endeavour, and it would be impossible to address in detail here every requirement for creating one. Instead, the aim is to provide a sense of opportunity and to signpost some of the practical tools and learning available to those with the ambition and vision to create exemplary new developments that truly merit the accolade 'garden city'.*

chapter 7

THE GARDEN CITY PRINCIPLES

Making new garden cities a reality means fusing the high social and environmental standards of the garden city movement with the highly effective delivery mechanisms of the new towns, incorporating the lessons learned about what has worked and what has not. To articulate what this means in practice, the TCPA identified a set of 'Garden City Principles', to provide a benchmark for the high ideals and standards necessary to achieve that ambition. This chapter provides an overview of these principles, as context for the remainder of Part 2.

What are the 'Garden City Principles'?

These nine principles (Box 7.01) distil the key elements that made the garden city model of development so successful, and apply them to the kinds of 21st-century challenges set out in Chapter 5. They incorporate approaches not only to design but also to delivery and governance, to articulate a fully integrated set of ideas for shaping a new kind of highly sustainable and mutualised way of living.

Land value capture for the benefit of the community

In the garden city financial model, capturing the uplift in land values that results from the development process provides a means to both pay down the debt of development and provide an asset base for future renewal and community benefit. **New garden cities should demonstrate how land values are captured for the benefit of the community**. Chapter 9 explores how to achieve this principle today.

Strong vision, leadership and community engagement

Britain's failure to designate a single large-scale new community for 50 years is partly to do with a lack of clear vision for the kinds of places we want to build, and partly shows a lack of political will to tackle significant delivery problems. Leadership at all levels is required in order to provide councils, delivery partners and the community with the assurances that they need to support the development, and to 'de-risk' the process enough to gain political support and investment. Ensuring that the process is underpinned by meaningful community engagement is fundamental to creating not only great places but places that will stand the test of time. **New garden cities should demonstrate a commitment to meaningful and ongoing community participation in the development process**. This principle provides a 'golden thread' throughout the following chapters.

Community ownership of land and long-term stewardship of assets

A new garden city requires a clear understanding of how the assets generated from the development process will be managed on behalf of the community. The stewardship task goes beyond the management of green space to the broadest range of garden city assets, including the active and positive management of commercial estates and utility companies. Putting local people at the heart of this process can generate increased local support, creativity and entrepreneurialism. **New garden cities should demonstrate how assets will be managed for the benefit of the community in perpetuity**. Chapter 10 explores this principle in more detail.

Mixed-tenure homes and housing types that are genuinely affordable

The garden cities were founded on an understanding of the importance of decent homes in high-quality environments for everyone. This means that new examples must have a primary focus on providing homes for those most in need in the current housing crisis. **As a benchmark, at least 30% of homes in a new garden city should be for social rent. Other forms of 'sub-market housing', such as shared equity and low-cost or discounted ownership, should apply to at least another 30%, with clear mechanisms to ensure that this arrangement is made available in perpetuity**. Housing mix and type is explored in more detail in Chapter 13.

A strong local jobs offer in the garden city itself, with a variety of employment opportunities within easy commuting distance of homes

While the changing nature of work means that the achievement of perfect employment self-sufficiency is impossible, and may in some circumstances not even be desirable, the aim should be to reduce the need to travel to work as far as is practicable. In practical terms, this means that while it will be vital to attract businesses to new garden cities it will also be important to ensure that new housing is designed to include enough space and the technical capacity for homeworking. **New garden cities must provide a full range of employment opportunities, with the aim of no less than one job per new household**. These spatial, financial and stewardship issues are explored in more detail in Chapters 8, 9 and 10, respectively.

Beautifully and imaginatively designed homes with gardens, combining the best of town and country to create healthy communities, and including opportunities to grow food

Garden cities should have beautiful homes, in attractive places, that are aesthetically, culturally and environmentally rich and stimulating – places of enduring quality. New garden cities must reflect the powerful role of art in people's lives, and the power of the natural environment to enhance wellbeing. This means high standards of design and sensitive use of materials and layout, contributing to local distinctiveness. **Ultimately, new garden cities must be beautiful places that lift the spirits of those that live there**.

The garden city vision was based on a belief that 'human society and the beauty of nature are meant to be enjoyed together'.[1] Its concept of 'town–country' was not only about combining the economic and social opportunities of urban and rural life but also about recognising the intrinsic beauty of the natural world and the benefits of experiencing nature for physical and psychological wellbeing. **New garden cities should meet Active Design guidelines in order to improve opportunities to access facilities for sport and physical activity**.[2] Chapter 14 explores this in more detail.

Development that enhances the natural environment, providing a comprehensive green infrastructure network and net biodiversity gains, and that uses zero-carbon and energy-positive technology to ensure climate resilience

Today, the intrinsic value of nature and biodiversity – as well as the range of social, physical and psychological benefits that it provides – is well evidenced, and consideration of these benefits forms a key policy priority. New garden cities should enable a net gain in local biodiversity, and plan to achieve the objectives of the Biodiversity 2020 strategy.[3] A defining characteristic of the original garden cities, Letchworth and Welwyn, is their setting of parks, open spaces, tree-lined streets and homes with generous gardens. **New garden cities must provide, as a minimum (and including private gardens), 50% of their total area as green space, of which at least half should be public and consist of a network of multifunctional, well-managed, high-quality green spaces linked to the wider countryside.** The role of green infrastructure is set out in further detail in Chapter 11.

Climate change is the greatest economic and social challenge facing society. In whatever sector we work, we should endeavour to forge practical and rapid paths to a sustainable low-carbon planet that now requires radical cuts in carbon emissions. Fairness and justice should be at the heart of the debate about how we respond. Climate resilience is multi-faceted, requiring the highest standards of environmental building and urban design. **New garden cities must be 'energy positive': by maximising opportunities for energy efficiency and renewable-energy generation, they should aim to produce more energy than they consume.** Climate change and energy are discussed further in Chapter 12.

Strong local cultural, recreational and shopping facilities in walkable neighbourhoods

The garden city movement placed great emphasis on the role of the arts and culture in improving wellbeing, as part of a cooperative approach to society. Garden cities should embrace cultural diversity and vibrancy, with design contributing to sociable neighbourhoods and recognising the needs of every resident. **New garden cities must provide a broad range of facilities – including space for social interaction, formal and informal cultural activities, sport and leisure – within walking distance of homes.** Chapter 14 explores the role of art and culture in further detail.

Integrated and accessible transport systems, with walking, cycling and public transport designed to be the most attractive forms of local transport, with a series of settlements linked by rapid transport

Integrated and accessible transport systems were central to Howard's garden city vision in two ways: first, in relation to the spatial development of a network of garden cities, linked by rapid transport to create the 'social city'; second, in terms of the physical walkability of neighbourhoods, to provide healthy lifestyles. Today's garden cities must consider how low-carbon rapid-transport systems can contribute to sustainable patterns of living, working and communicating. They should embrace the latest low-and zero-carbon technologies, and aim over time to be free of polluting vehicles. Those planning them should look at key lessons from continental Europe in relation to transport planning. **The garden city's design must enable at least 50% of trips originating there to be made my non-car means, with a goal to increase this over time to at least 60%, and must**

use the latest best practice in street and transport design as a minimum standard.[4] Chapter 10 sets out the need for a transport network that makes walking, cycling and public transport the most attractive modes of travel.

A Framework for Good Place-making

It is important to remember the holistic objective of these principles. Taken together they form an indivisible and interlocking framework for the delivery of high-quality places (Fig 7.01). If applied to a new development on its own, each principle will be beneficial – but only developments that incorporate *all* of the principles can be truly described as 'garden cities', and are likely to become more desirable – not less – as time passes. This partly reflects the holistic vision of the garden city pioneers but it also has a direct, practical effect. For example, capturing land values is vital to securing the wider social and environmental outcomes for people in perpetuity, and providing a comprehensive green-infrastructure network, walkable neighbourhoods and prioritising public transport is vital to achieving healthy, sociable, low-carbon communities.

Applying the Principles to New Development

The garden city principles are not a 'blueprint' for new development, but an approach to design and delivery. New garden cities shouldn't replicate the Letchworth and Welwyn experiments, but should use the principles as a foundation for innovation in new ways of living. This will be expressed differently at every site, reflecting the unique circumstances of each particular project and place. The key to successful application of the principles is considering them early, and having in place the right delivery body and mechanisms to make them a reality – at the development stage, and into the future. The following chapters set out how the principles can be applied in the creation of sustainable new garden cities. ◆

Fig 7.01
The 'garden city principles' form an indivisible and interlocking framework for good place-making.

chapter 8

LOCATION AND PLANNING CONSENT

New garden cities cannot be achieved without access to the right land, in the right place, at the right price. The garden city pioneers and their development companies were able to identify the desired agricultural land, purchase it at auction and get on with building their utopia as quickly as resources would allow.

Today, the procedure is far more complex. The process of identifying the need for, and potential locations of, new garden cities (or, indeed, any new community) takes place within a planning system informed by development plans, and projects require planning approval through a democratic consent process. In theory this should lead to better outcomes, but this requires strong national policy on the creation of development plans and the subsequent identification of new communities. In England at present, this policy environment is both confused and dysfunctional. The benefits of large-scale development and the garden city principles are currently recognised in national policy, but without a national framework for the identification of locations for new large-scale housing developments – or, indeed, for housing at any scale.

This chapter explores the options currently available for finding sites and getting planning permission for new garden cities in this policy context, and sets out how a national, strategic approach to identifying a programme of new garden cities might work today.

Criteria for Locating New Garden Cities

Identifying the need for, and locations of, successful new developments that adhere to the garden city principles requires consideration of a complex web of factors at a range of geographical and temporal scales. The right approach will vary from place to place, but common approaches and criteria can be used to guide site identification anywhere.

Organisational approach

Any authority undertaking a site-selection process must commit to advocacy, collaborative working, long-term perspective and strong evidence-based policy-making:

Strong local leadership

The initiation and long-term success of any large-scale development project requires the enthusiasm and commitment of local leaders in order to engage local people from the outset, building trust in an often challenging process. Once a project is permitted, the delivery period of the new community will extend far beyond several electoral cycles – and will, in fact, benefit future generations not currently represented in the political process. Larger-scale projects coming forward in places like Bicester and Northstowe have benefitted from strong leadership and advocacy from local councillors, who have helped to build confidence and drive delivery.

Thinking beyond the Local Plan boundary

Unless an authority is large in its territory or unitary in its powers, the need for a garden city and potential locations for growth are likely to cross administrative boundaries. Even where this is not the case, and particularly in the absence of formal regional structures, authorities will need to plan together to consider impacts on local infrastructure and services. There are a number of emerging routes to achieve this. Cooperation between councils (as required by the 'Duty to Co-operate') should be undertaken from an early stage, not only to identify a strategy for growth and share resources but also to coordinate engagement with existing communities (Case Study 8.01). Strategic planning carried out through, for example, joint planning committees can reduce costs, promote efficiency and lessen conflict, while protecting the environment and promoting development in the right places.

Taking a long-term view of growth requirements

The challenge for local authorities is to determine the best long-term solution to ensure that the appropriate amount of growth is planned for (Case Study 8.02). This means thinking in at least 20- to 30-year timescales rather than in terms of the five-year housing-supply requirements set out in the current planning system. This includes considering the right pattern and scale of development; this may involve regenerating existing areas, or creating sustainable urban extensions or new settlements – and ensuring enough land is considered from the outset. Though land will be brought forward in phases over a long period of time, this can help to ensure better long-term planning of other developments, such as transport infrastructure and services.

Evidence base

The process of identifying locations for new garden cities (or, indeed, whether they are the right solution at all) should be underpinned by a strong evidence base. This requires a range of assessments, including evaluations of housing requirements, urban capacity (for example, strategic housing land availability assessments), employment, the economy, flood risk, transport, biodiversity, landscape

▶ CASE STUDY 8.01

NORTH NORTHAMPTONSHIRE JOINT PLANNING UNIT

The North Northamptonshire JPU demonstrates how thinking beyond the Local Plan boundary can prove beneficial and efficient in services terms. The JPU was formally established in October 2004 by Corby, Kettering, Wellingborough and East Northamptonshire councils, together with Northamptonshire County Council. It is funded through contributions from the local planning authorities, and coordinates the preparation of the North Northamptonshire Local Plan. The Joint Planning Committee (JPC) was established in July 2005 as the JPU's formal decision-making body, and was the first such committee established under new planning legislation. It comprises three elected members from each council, and is responsible for agreeing the Joint Core Spatial Strategy ('the Plan') and other joint planning-policy work, but has no development control powers (these remain with the individual district/borough councils).

The Plan was adopted in June 2008, and provides a framework for long-term change and development in North Northamptonshire, including housing, jobs, retail and the environment. It also has policies to guide how change will be managed – such as, where development should be located, guidelines about its design and controls over the impacts of development sites on their surroundings, and any infrastructure needing to be provided. In 2016, the Plan is in the process of being reviewed, and the JPU is working on a Joint Core Strategy that includes housing requirements and strategic opportunities: development principles for strategic sites. Based on the framework provided by the Plan, the individual councils are working to prepare more detailed plans for parts of their areas, including site-specific proposals, policies to control the form of development and area action plans for the town centres.[2]

Fig 8.01
Prior's Hall, Corby.

and energy-production needs and capacity. At an early stage, the key tools for informing the plan-making process – and the Local Plan's approach to future growth – include Sustainability Appraisal, incorporating Strategic Environmental Assessment (SA/SEA). Using the evidence base described above, these tools can determine the broad spatial locations for future growth, including whether a large-scale new community or garden city is the most sustainable option. Larger-scale developments in places like Wokingham have emerged from such a process. Unfortunately, tools such as Sustainability Appraisal are often used as a procedural afterthought rather than a useful tool for options assessment.

Understanding spatial patterns of growth

One of the key benefits of new garden cities is that they can help to prevent the sprawl of existing towns and villages by providing strategic locations for sustainable new growth. When considering options for growth, it is often thought cheaper – and politically easier – to link into the existing physical and social infrastructure of a place rather than creating a new, but connected, community. However, no matter how rationally efficient and economical (and relatively easy) it might be to supplement a town with another housing estate, suburb, business park or 'sustainable urban extension', that town must eventually reach its limit (see Box 8:01). This limit might

▶ CASE STUDY 8.02

IMAGINING THE FUTURE IN MILTON KEYNES

Milton Keynes is a unitary authority, which includes one of the fastest-growing cities in the country: the new town of Milton Keynes. Since its designation as a new town in 1967, Milton Keynes has been considered keen to 'go for growth'. Having already reached its planned population of 250,000, the city is set to double in size through a series of planned urban extensions. The council is currently working on a new Local Plan for the town – called Plan:MK, taking a 15-year view – which will replace the 2013 Core Strategy. Alongside the Local Plan processes, the council is also taking a longer-term perspective and has set up an 'MK Futures 2050 Commission' to engage and explore what it means to make a great city greater – discussing what factors could affect Milton Keynes over the coming decades, and the

possible future scenarios that could be created when thinking about those drivers. This includes considering different spatial options for growth – from further expansion to a cluster of smaller garden cities around the new town. The findings of the commission will be used to inform the strategic development options in the Local Plan. Having a process which looks at long-term growth options alongside Local Plan processes allows the council to think beyond that document's timescales, and having an independent commission adds an additional layer of rigour to the consideration of development options. However, setting up such a body can be costly, so may not be an option for all councils. There must also be clarity on how the commission will work with local people, to ensure a legitimate process.

Box 8.01: What about garden suburbs and sustainable urban extensions?

The · Garden · City · Principle · applied · to · Suburbs.

Mr Raymond Unwin here illustrates the application of the Garden City principle to a belt of green encircling the whole community to the extension of new Suburbs. The Suburbs are seen separated from the City by belts of land which will remain open for all time.

Reproduced from " The Garden City Movement Up-to-Date " by Ewart G. Culpin. Copies obtainable from the Garden Cities and Town Planning Association, 3 Gray's Inn Place, W.C., or Messrs P. S. King & Son, Orchard House, Great Smith Street, Westminster, S.W.

Garden City principles can be applied at a range of scales. Sustainable urban extensions have been a popular approach to accommodating new development. The benefits of linking into existing infrastructure networks, such as transport, jobs and social infrastructure, include lower short-term costs. Furthermore, depending on the site, sustainable urban extensions are sometimes perceived to have fewer environmental impacts. However, unless they are properly planned, urban extensions can result in 'bolt-on estates', as ambitions fall away over time from the original vision. In practice, such bolt-on estates can encourage increased car use as they are usually little more than dormitories, often without an economic or community centre. However, well planned garden suburbs or urban villages could address these possible failings if they follow the principles set out in Chapter 7 as part of a 'garden communities' palette of options.

Fig 8.03
The garden city prinicples applied to suburbs – Raymond Unwin's vision of garden suburbs in 1912 caused fierce debate among the garden city 'purists'.

be a physical boundary or feature in the landscape, or it may be 'just the sense – which could actually be measured ... that the latest town expansion is so removed from the heart of the place that it might as well not be part of the place at all'.[3] In high-growth areas – and especially where green belts have been designated, adding a policy stop to what may be a physical or psychological one – the choice may have to be made between hugely expanding a small town or village nearby and starting a whole new town, using the evidence base to understand the right solution. A whole portfolio of solutions to meeting growth needs is necessary, and the correct one may be different in each case. What is important is to understand that the easiest route might not be the right one, and to ensure that the whole range of solutions has been considered. Councils should take a leading role in site selection, considering a range of them – not just those promoted by the private sector through a call for sites.

Good connectivity

New garden cities cannot be stand-alone, and will always form part of the existing network of development across the country. In the 21st century, it is not only undesirable but also impossible to create a 'self-contained' place. The postwar new towns were tasked with this aim, and it was never possible to achieve it; a location that is well connected physically and economically is essential. The garden city pioneers recognised the importance of connection, with their concept of the 'social city' demonstrating the benefits of a cluster of smaller settlements, linked by rapid public transport, which together provide the benefits of a much larger place. In 2007, the TCPA set out how existing transport corridors could be used to identify locations for linked new settlements.[4] Peter Hall and Colin Ward explored this in detail in their book *Sociable Cities*,[5] setting out proposals for new developments in the Midlands, the east of England and the south-east, and explaining how developing

Fig 8.04
The masterplan for Peter Halls'
'city of Mercia', with two 'social
city' clusters - Daventry Magna
and Rugby garden cities.

in strategic locations along existing road
and rail routes could provide a sustainable
pattern of growth and also protect rural
areas away from these routes (Fig 8.03).
The right spatial approach may be different
in each area, but those considering
different patterns of growth should always
look first at connectivity.

Opportunities for sustainable development

Locations for new garden cities should
not only avoid damaging areas that are
protected for their ecological, landscape,
historical or climate-resilience value but
should also actively be located in areas
where there can be a positive impact
on these assets. Underpinning the
consideration of sites for new garden cities
should be the extent to which each one will
allow for

▶ resource use within environmental limits
– by avoiding areas of water stress,
for example;

▶ the achievement of social justice –
ie providing genuinely affordable
homes and a variety of employment
opportunities in areas of need; and

▶ positive impacts on biodiversity and
assets of ecological, landscape, historical
and climate-resilience value – eg where
a development could help to enhance
green infrastructure or make links in a
habitat 'mosaic' or corridor.

Opportunities for bridging regional economic inequalities

In recent years, the focus of large-scale
development has been primarily in the
south-east of England. While this responds
to identified need, it does not consider
the impacts on the economic geography
of the country as a whole and the need
to 'rebalance' it. Processes for identifying
locations for new garden cities should
consider this wider geography.[6]

The Government's Current Approach

In the absence of a national or regional strategy for growth, the onus is on local authorities to identify the need for new communities through their Local Plan processes. These should be guided by the principles and criteria set out above, but a lack of resources and pressure to draft plans at speed mean that this is not always possible. Without a government requirement to consider these issues, it is up to progressive local authorities to take this approach.

Several authorities are going for growth using their Local Plan. There are also a number of larger-scale developments coming forward that were not identified in Local Plans. Many of these sites have been in the planning process for some time, and include four of those that received support under the Labour Government's eco-towns programme (Fig 8.05). As set out in Chapter 6, a number of projects are also receiving support through the government's 'locally led garden cities, towns and villages' programme.

Despite these initiatives, there are simply not enough sites coming forward of the right scale, in the right places, or which compare well with the garden city ideal. Numbers aside, relying solely on Local Plan processes does not enable a strategic approach to the identification of locations. The duty to cooperate, which was created in the Localism Act 2011 and in theory encourages local authorities to work across boundaries, has proved to be generally ineffective. Potential receptors of growth arising elsewhere tend to be unwilling to collaborate. The current approach is also not delivering quickly enough. Even when the need has been identified, it takes a significant amount of time – sometimes decades – to obtain permission for the site and to get building. The project at

Fig 8.05
Map of projects that have received support under the locally led garden villages, towns and cities initiative as of March 2017

Garden Villages
1   Long Marston (Stratford-on-Avon)
2   Oxfordshire Cotswold (West Oxfordshire)
3   Deenethorpe (East Northamptonshire)
4   Culm (Mid Devon)
5   Welbourne (Fareham)
6   West Carclaze (Cornwall)
7   Dunton Hills (Brentwood)
8   Spitalgate Heath (South Kesteven)
9   Halsnead (Knowsley)
10 Longcross (Runnymeade and Surrey Heath)
11 Bailrigg (Lancaster)
12 Infinity Garden Village (South Derbyshire and Derby City)
13 Handforth (Cheshire East)
14 St Cuthberts (Carlisle)

Garden Towns
1   Ebbsfleet
2   Otterpool Park (Kent)
3   Bicester
4   Basingstoke
5   Didcot
6   North Essex (Colchester, Braintree, Tending)
7   North Northamptonshire
8   Aylesbury
9   Taunton
10 Harlow and Gilston

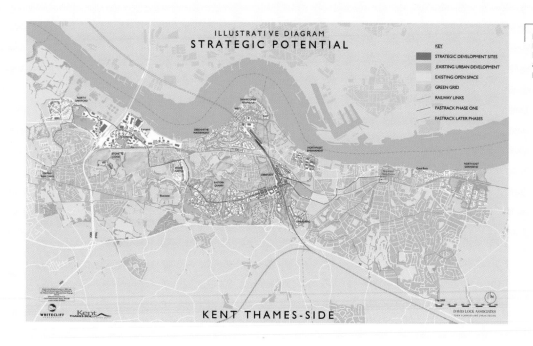

ILLUSTRATIVE DIAGRAM
STRATEGIC POTENTIAL

KENT THAMES-SIDE

Fig 8.06
Kent Thames-side
Masterplan 1998: the project
at Ebbsfleet has been in
planning for over 20 years.

Ebbsfleet in Kent, for example, has, as of 2016, been in the planning system for over 20 years (Fig 8.06).

In addition, where existing projects already have planning permission, or are some way through the plan-making process, and are 'rebranded' as a garden city, the potential to implement the full range of garden city principles is reduced.

What is missing is a clear planning mechanism for the identification of sites linked to planning consent for new garden cities that forms part of a broader, spatial approach open to a portfolio of solutions needed to meet the nation's housing requirements.

The Recommended Approach

While the first garden cities did not require planning permission, the New Towns Act instituted a consent process that took in some cases as little as three months and on average about three years – significantly faster than today's processes. Within the current legislative landscape, there are broadly two possible routes available for obtaining consent for new garden cities.[7]

The first is to continue using existing Local Plan and development-management processes. Identifying new garden cities through Local Plan processes and using existing planning-permission procedures allows for a thorough and democratically accountable process. However, for the reasons set out above this is unlikely to lead to sites coming forward at a fast enough speed, in the right place or at the scale necessary to meet our housing needs.

The second route available is to create a specific consent regime for new garden cities. The New Towns Act demonstrated how a dedicated consent regime could allow for the speedy designation of new communities (much faster than today's system). A consent regime for new garden cities would need to be predicated by

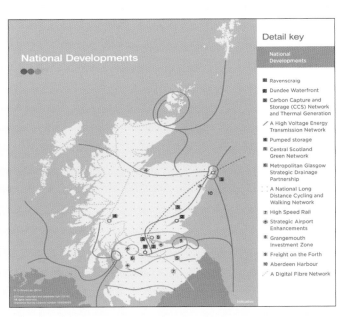

National Developments

Detail key

National
Developments

- Ravenscraig
- Dundee Waterfront
- Carbon Capture and
  Storage (CCS) Network
  and Thermal Generation
- A High Voltage Energy
  Transmission Network
- Pumped storage
- Central Scotland
  Green Network
- Metropolitan Glasgow
  Strategic Drainage
  Partnership
- A National Long
  Distance Cycling and
  Walking Network
- High Speed Rail
- Strategic Airport
  Enhancements
- Grangemouth
  Investment Zone
- Freight on the Forth
- Aberdeen Harbour
- A Digital Fibre Network

Fig 8.07
The National Framework for
Scotland, 2014; England is
the only UK 'nation' to have
no national spatial-planning
framework.

duty to cooperate – which has produced some very mixed results.[8] Without a wider geographical perspective, it is impossible to consider the key locational criteria outlined earlier in this chapter.

Today, what is needed is for nationally or regionally expressed policy to decide the number, scale and broad areas of search for the location of new settlements, thus providing the context for local decision-making. One approach would be for the government to identify 'areas of search' for new garden cities. The relevant local authority, or group of authorities, would then approach the minister, present the evidence base, and ask him or her to use the New Towns Act to designate the area and create a development corporation. The support of the Department for Communities and Local Government (DCLG), as sponsoring department – and of the Treasury and neighbouring authorities, and statutory bodies and agencies – would have been nurtured as the locally led planning process unfolded.

There is a recent precedent in the growth area studies for national policy that provided focused areas of search to support decision-making, as set out in Chapter 4. If taken forward, this policy would need to consider the wider spatial role of new communities in the context of the nation as whole – including the relationship of such communities to future infrastructure provision and resource use. A national policy would also need to provide some detail on governance standards and the operation of development corporations, and establish broad expectations in terms of design and technology.

It is extremely important for the legitimacy of the designation process that such a policy should have parliamentary approval. The lesson of recent history is that strategic approaches to growth that do not have democratic endorsement are liable to be very short-lived. Approval under such a

a local-authority-led process of site identification, and be a democratically robust and transparent process. With this second route in mind, it is worth exploring how the New Towns Act could be modernised to provide a suitable consent mechanism for new garden cities.

A national spatial plan and updated New Towns Act

One of the key lessons to be drawn from past experience is that successful approaches to delivering new communities – such as the new towns programme – were set within a strong national-policy framework – for example, the dispersal of population from London or Glasgow.

Unlike Scotland (Fig 8.07), Wales and Northern Ireland, England does not have a national strategic plan, nor any level of strategic planning above the local-authority level (with the exception of Greater London, and in some cases the 'Combined Authorities' emerging from the devolution agenda). Instead, councils must rely on the

1. Creation of a national spatial plan for housing based on a sound evidence base, underpinned by key locational criteria and garden city principles; the plan would identify areas of search and set out a dedicated consent mechanism for new garden cities.

2. Local authorities, or groups of local authorities, within the areas of search would then undertake needs and site-assessment studies and set out a design brief for the sequential testing of sites (the brief would be consulted on).

3. A public inquiry would be undertaken on the shortlisted site/s, including in its remit the most appropriate delivery vehicle.

4. The site would be designated, and a garden city development corporation created (where this has been identified as the most appropriate delivery vehicle).

policy might be modelled on the process for preparing national planning statements set out in the Planning Act 2008. There would also be a need for a strong, supportive relationship with the government, requiring an experienced and motivated team within central government that could secure interdepartmental agreements.

An outline of the suggested stages for locating and permitting a new garden city is provided in Box 8.02.

The Reality in March 2017

Despite the 2017 Housing White Paper indicating government's renewed interest in strategic planning and updating the New Towns Act, a national strategic approach to locating and permitting new garden cities is, at the time of writing, still some way off. In its absence, it is up to local authorities, developers and communities to work together to decide on the most suitable location and size needed to provide a sustainable community that creates jobs, meets local housing need, and finances and supports the necessary hard and soft infrastructure required for a community to thrive.

Local authorities can work alone to plan for growth through Local Plan processes, work jointly with adjacent authorities (eg where they share a Housing Market Area or have created a Joint Planning Unit) or work as a 'Combined Authority'.

At present, for all of these scenarios the process of obtaining planning permission for a development must take place through the current development-management system. Whatever shape the authority undertaking this agenda, there are tried and tested approaches for analysis alongside the Local Plan-making process. This may involve a full or partial Local Plan review, involving stages of evidence-based analysis to establish growth needs (including a long-term view to 'future-proof' requirements) and an assessment of all reasonable spatial options for development, including new settlements. From the outset, the local authority should establish a comprehensive strategy for meaningful and ongoing public engagement, but should stage a formal consultation on preferred options.[9] The process should be underpinned by the garden city principles and locational considerations set out in this chapter, and include early consideration of the form of local delivery body and land ownership.

The planning authority also has a fundamental role to play in securing control of the land. The ideal solution is for the authority to establish a delivery vehicle that acquires the land through negotiation or compulsory purchase. New 'locally-accountable' development corporations provide a new route for this. The form of this local delivery body, and the management/governance structures involved, will vary from one garden city location to another, but it should be determined through a process of open discussion between key delivery partners. It may be formed by the local authority and make use of many of their existing processes. The different types and requirements for different local delivery bodies, and the relationship between delivery and finance, are set out in the following chapter. ◆

chapter 9

FINANCE AND DELIVERY

Part 1 of this book demonstrated the importance and practicality of creating very high-quality, inclusive places that can meet our national housing needs. Delivering on this ambition means having a sound financial model able to deal with the basic up-front costs of land and infrastructure, as well as placing funds in the hands of a suitable body to manage it for the long-term development and renewal of the community. It also means having a delivery body that can provide leadership and certainty in the development process, de-risking development for the community and investors. Financial feasibility, including the cost of borrowing, is directly related to the kind of delivery vehicle that is employed to build new places. The 'master developer' must have the vision, public legitimacy, institutional support and financial backing to drive the complex job of place-making.

This chapter outlines the opportunities for financing new garden cities and how this relates to delivery, including how modernised new town development corporations may be the most effective model for achieving efficient delivery and a sound financial model.

The Financial Foundation of New Garden Cities

Understanding approaches to financing new garden cities requires that we learn from the original experiments and the financial flexibility, but also vulnerability of the postwar new towns (both explored in Part 1). Land-value capture, as set out in Chapter 3, remains an important part of the finance and delivery of new garden cities. In today's context, there are three core principles that underpin this financial model (Box 9.01):

These three core principles of the garden city financial model are explored further below.

Capturing and sharing the uplift in land values

It is important to understand that land-value uplift is one of several sources of value generation arising from the development process. The primary sources of value generated by the creation of new garden cities are:

▶ Value resulting from the action of public authorities in granting planning permission and investing in infrastructure – known as 'betterment'.[2] Betterment increases the value of land, and currently benefits private landowners (even where they haven't contributed to the creation of that value).[3]

▶ Rental and sales incomes from the residential and commercial estate, as the garden city is developed – a model still employed successful at Letchworth (Fig 9.01).

▶ Income from locally controlled facilities and utilities and the provision of key services, such as energy supply.

Box 9.01: Core principles of land-value capture

1. The opportunity for capturing and sharing the uplift in land values that development creates is vital in delivering the garden city principles. Landowners may well receive a premium for their land in order to facilitate negotiated sales, but this should not compromise the viability of the wider scheme in terms of debt repayment or the long-term security of community assets.

2. Capturing land values on this basis requires a delivery body with land-assembly and compulsory-purchase[1] powers. While it is possible for a local authority to engage in this task (as many continental European municipalities do), years of financial cuts have led to a real skills and capacity shortfall. The delivery body should also constitute, or make provision for, a longer-term stewardship body.

3. Effective delivery mechanisms, including the right delivery body, can de-risk the development process, allowing for long-term, 'patient' investment in new garden cities from the public and private sectors. Because the first two land-value-capture principles effectively secure investor confidence, it is possible to consider financing garden cities through a mixture of private and public funds.

Fig 9.01
Letchworth's financial model means it is able to reinvest £4m a year in the town through charitable initiatives.

These sources present an opportunity for long-term income streams that can support future investment in the community. For example, continental European cities such as Malmö and Hamburg (Fig 9.02) derive substantial income from municipal energy companies. Germany has a large number of community-owned energy cooperatives (its National Association of Energy Cooperatives represents around 700 of them), which allow for genuine local control of energy investment.

Capturing land values

Land is the most critical factor in the production of place. Land economy is therefore one of the most vital, but often opaque, parts of the development process. Viability assessments (see Chapter 13)[4] and land valuation are often overlaid with commercial confidentially, which can make it extremely difficult to judge the merits or otherwise of land deals and development proposals – and understand who is benefitting from the 'betterment' that results from the planning and development process.

Perhaps the most straightforward way to capture land values is to tax them. While betterment taxation is a feature of many continental European development systems, it remains an aspiration in Britain since land taxes were abolished in 1985. The current position is complex, with a number of marginal ways of recouping some development value through the planning process. The most widely used approach is through planning obligations and strong policy requirements for developers. For example, setting robust policy requirements for affordable homes or zero-carbon buildings is a way of achieving high-quality policy outcomes for the public. Theoretically, this should depress land prices as developers seek to maintain their profit margins. Local government can also negotiate contributions from developers. Planning obligations through Section 106 ('s106') agreements (named after that section of the Town and Country Planning Act 1990) and Community Infrastructure Levy contributions are derived from development values, and can be used for public benefit.

Betterment can also be used to unlock up-front infrastructure investment. One of the notable frameworks for achieving this was pioneered at Milton Keynes in the form of Strategic Land and Infrastructure Contracts (SLICs – agreements between public- and private-sector partners to commit to investment and development activities in order to de-risk the process for both parties).[5] There are also councils, such as North Essex, who are exploring new ways to use their control of the development process in order to capture and share development values (Case Study 9.01).

▶ **CASE STUDY 9.01**

NORTH ESSEX – EXPLORING NEW APPROACHES TO SHARING LAND VALUES

Fig 9.03
Essex Business School at the University of Essex, which could provide employment for new garden communnities.

As part of a cross-boundary project considering the role of new communities to meet housing needs, Colchester, Braintree and Tendring borough councils, together with Essex County Council, are looking beyond the Local Plan to consider the delivery of new settlements. The 'North Essex Garden Settlements' project has received funding from the Department for Communities and Local Government, and includes joint-governance arrangements that will be periodically reviewed as developments progress. This includes creating a single Shadow Joint Delivery Board for Garden Communities, and a Garden Communities Joint Steering Group. As the projects are at a very early stage, there is an opportunity to explore options for capturing land values on the sites. As well as working with Essex University and the Advisory Team for Large Applications (ATLAS – part of the Homes and Communities Agency), the councils have jointly commissioned Garden City Developments CIC, a not-for-profit community interest company, to promote and establish partnerships with local landowners and option holders to investigate the feasibility of the proposed garden settlements. Discussions with relevant parties have been used to develop the councils' options around applying land-value capture and long-term stewardship arrangements. They also specifically explore landowners' appetites for engaging with the councils on these issues, and their willingness to enter into legally binding agreements to this effect in return for better certainty of delivery without lengthy s106 negotiations. The aim is to put the councils in the position of 'master developer' by having effective control or ownership of the land, and giving more control of the quality and type of development that is brought forward, as well as an ability to retain a legitimate share in the increases in land values as projects are built. The North Essex Garden Settlements project is visionary in its aims, and constantly evolving. This shows the importance of capacity funding from the government to enable these discussions and investigation of options to take place – as well as the need for strong local leadership and cooperation, to think strategically over the long term.

There is one common feature of all approaches to development and land-value capture: they require a strong planning and delivery body capable of negotiating from a position of strength, and backed by enough resources to be effective and by compulsory purchase powers to be used as last resort to bring landowners to the table. There must be control, if not outright ownership, of the land to be able to capture land values and share them by reinvesting in the ongoing development process and in community development.

Finding the right delivery vehicle

If the financial credibility of a new garden city is dependent on the confidence investors feel over long-term delivery, then that delivery has to be backed by a body that ensures that the job gets done. New garden cities should be large-scale, innovative, long-term developments, aiming for the highest standards of sustainability and inclusion. Managing their delivery cannot be left to chance. Regardless of the number of organisations involved in delivering the individual components of the garden city, visible leadership and responsibility for project management needs to be vested in one body. The role of this organisation, sometimes referred to as a local delivery vehicle or local delivery body, should include:

▶ consistent leadership in driving forward delivery of the vision;

▶ commitment to the garden city principles;

▶ developing and 'owning' a business plan for delivery that identifies the responsibilities of each partner, including clear timelines for action;

▶ securing the funding to deliver the business plan;

▶ brokering agreements with, and cajoling delivery by, its partners – including the use of statutory powers, where appropriate (eg compulsory purchase, and planning);

▶ monitoring overall progress;

▶ working in a transparent, participative and accountable manner that engenders confidence and inclusiveness;

▶ communicating effectively and transparently with all parts of the community; and

▶ ownership or control of the land.

Local delivery vehicles come in a variety of forms – from powerful and nationally supported new town development corporations, modernised to meet the needs of today, on the one hand, to grassroots-initiated Community Land Trusts (CLTs) that may control all of a smaller site or part of a new garden city on the other. The role of councils and the private sector varies with the models in between.

Establishing a local delivery vehicle

While modernised new town development corporations offer the most readily available and proven model for creating new garden cities, the exact form of local delivery body and the governance structures involved will vary from one location to another. They should be determined through a process of open discussion based on genuine community participation. The delivery body may be formed by the local authority, and make use of many of their existing processes. A local delivery vehicle needs to be given clear responsibility and sufficient authority, and the resources to get on with its day-to-day job. This needs to be conducted within a framework created by agreement between its partners, expressed in a masterplan and through its business plan. As a result of the Localism Act 2011, councils now have a powerful general power of competence, which gives greater confidence in undertaking commercial partnerships through development companies.

Development corporations

Development corporations provide the most powerful form of delivery body, combining all the aforementioned functions with strong statutory planning powers. There are three kinds of development-corporation approach:

▶ New town development corporations (NTDCs);

▶ Urban development corporations (UDCs); and

▶ Mayoral development corporations (MDCs), which can now also be used by Combined Authorities.

All these models have similar characteristics in terms of planning and delivery powers, but with some important differences (Table 9.01). The first is objectives and scale; UDCs and MDCs are designed for the purposes of regenerating an existing urban development area, whereas NTDCs are specifically tailored to delivering large-scale new communities. All three are able to take on development-management powers, such as the ability to determine planning applications, but in practice NTDCs are the only body with statutory plan-making powers. At present, MDCs are the only one of the three not to be designated by the Secretary of State. New 'locally accountable' development corporations, made possible through an amended New Towns Act, are likely to remain designated by the Secretary of State, though the request to designate, and the accountability of the corporation when designated would rest with the local Responsible Body' (which may be a local authority or group of local authorities).

TABLE 9.01:
COMPARISON OF DEVELOPMENT-CORPORATION MODELS

	OBJECTIVES AND SCALE	DESIGNATION & ACCOUNTABILITY	PLANNING POWERS	OTHER POWERS	RECENT EXAMPLES
NEW TOWN DEVELOPMENT CORPORATIONS	Delivering large-scale new communities within a designated development area	Designated by, and accountable to, the secretary of state Legislation due to be amended in 2017 to introduce a parallel route for creation of 'locally accountable' Development Corporations where accountability rests with a Responsible Body' other than the Secretary of State	Comprehensive plan-making powers and development-management powers	Powers to acquire, compulsory purchase and develop land and infrastructure	The last NTDC was wound up in 1996
URBAN DEVELOPMENT CORPORATIONS	Regenerating a specific, designated urban-development area	Designated by, and accountable to, the secretary of state	Limited plan-making powers and development-management powers	Powers to acquire, compulsory purchase and develop land and infrastructure	Ebbsfleet UDC Olympic Delivery Authority
MAYORAL DEVELOPMENT CORPORATIONS	Regenerating a specific, designated urban-development area	Designated by, and accountable to, the relevant mayor	Limited plan-making powers and development-management powers	Powers to acquire, compulsory purchase and develop land and infrastructure	Old Oak and Park Royal Development Corporation

As explored in Chapter 3, history shows that NTDCs are the best way of delivering new places as they have extensive legal powers to get the job done. UDCs – and, more recently, MDCs – are useful for the specific task of regeneration but do not have the breadth of powers and objectives for the complex and long-term task of making a whole new community. The government's recent support for a

UDC at Ebbsfleet in Kent (Case Study 9.02) demonstrates the benefits, but also the challenges, of identifying a delivery body at a late stage in the development process. However, NTDCs are not perfect; they also need critical modernisation and, in particular, a clear statutory purpose that can ensure their powers are used responsibly. What is necessary is a broader set of visionary objectives for development

▶ CASE STUDY 9.02

EBBSFLEET URBAN DEVELOPMENT CORPORATION

In the 2014 Budget, the government announced a £310m package of support to help realise existing plans for the development of Ebbsfleet, a site in north Kent. This included the use of an Urban Development Corporation (UDC) to drive delivery on the site. The UDC was established on 1 July 2015, and the vision is for 15,000 homes – of which, 11,200 already have planning permission. The UDC is working with developers, and is the planning authority for the development. It has been working with communities on a new vision for the area and a set of design principles to guide future development. Ebbsfleet is being promoted as a 'garden city', but the UDC has made no 'constitutional' commitment to the garden city principles, and the government has made clear that it does not aim to get ownership of the land. Given this lack of land ownership, and the fact that the majority of homes have already been permitted (and therefore s106 agreements are already in place), it will be very challenging to achieve garden city principles such as land-value capture. However, there is no doubt that the presence of a specific delivery vehicle in the form of the UDC, backed by government financial support to invest in key infrastructure projects and drive delivery, has helped to unlock development at this strategic location in the south-east.

Fig 9.04
Aerial overview of Ebsfleet.

corporations, which reflects their wider place-making role and includes a much stronger focus on social justice, public participation and climate change – ensuring partnership working with the established local authorities in the area in which the new town is located, and the timely handover of the new town's assets (ie land, property, finance) to the local authorities and to other successor bodies to hold and manage in perpetuity for the benefit of the community.[6]

Community-led delivery vehicles

Direct community control through establishing a Community Land Trust (CLT) is a potential way of securing greater community ownership of, and control over, the quality of a development. Among other things, a CLT can reserve land for social housing, develop it and hold the land in perpetuity. Rather than the normal options of renting or shared ownership, this would open up opportunities for more mutual forms of tenure. A CLT could also own the public realm; run energy, water and waste services companies; provide community-development services; and own local commercial properties. CLTs have no fixed legal form – they can be companies limited by guarantee, cooperatives or other forms of organisation capable of owning and managing assets on behalf of the community. Community-led development models are explored further in Chapter 10.

Linking delivery and long-term stewardship

Whichever type of delivery vehicle is used for a new garden city, it will need to determine at an early stage how the assets of the new community will be managed in perpetuity. The delivery vehicle may become the stewardship body after a certain point, or may create a related or subsidiary body for this purpose (for example, a CLT). These links are explored further in Chapter 10.

Unlocking 'patient' investment

The third core principle of land-value capture today is that the right delivery vehicle provides the certainty necessary to unlock investment from the public and private sector.

Public-sector investment in new garden cities

In the past, the central government has offered direct investment through long-term low-rate loans and redirected wider investment streams on housing and infrastructure to fund new settlements – as was the case for the new towns programme.

In 2017, although Government has committed to updating the New Towns Act to support locally-led delivery, this has not been accompanied by new government investment approaches, and important issues over how to strike a fair balance between landowners and taxpayers in compensation deals have yet to be resolved. As highlighted in Chapter 6, the government has backed new urban development corporations (UDCs) such that as at Ebbsfleet, but it has made clear that it, in general, does not wish to commit resources to supply-side housing investment.

Localism and the devolution process have led to a different pattern of local government and financing in Britain, and the government is instead seeking to strike bespoke financial deals over some locally led proposals. Where groups of neighbouring local authorities have united to form Combined Authorities, such as the 10 Greater Manchester councils that have come together to form the Greater Manchester Combined Authority, they will have growing control over what was previously national departmental spend and will receive planning powers, including the power to designate a Mayoral Development Corporation (MDC). Not only do new Combined Authorities potentially represent a form of strategic planning for housing growth but MDCs might become the preferred route for designation of new communities. With a lack of government focus on supply-side investment, there is clearly a need to link public and private finance in order to unlock the delivery of new garden cities.

Private-sector investment in new garden cities

In essence, there are two related sources of investment from the private sector. First, private money invested directly in housing and commercial development, including building for sale or rent. This began to happen in the final generation of new towns, and allows a master developer (such as a development corporation) to select a private partner to invest and deliver part of a masterplan. This does not, however, deal with vital up-front costs or land acquisition and infrastructure provision. The second source is long-term, 'patient' investment (normally assumed to be of institutional finance) looking for a direct trade-off between lower returns and investment certainty. Such public/private joint ventures are well established in relation to regeneration and infrastructure, and there is undoubtedly a commercial opportunity in the development of new communities. This model relies on not just a powerful delivery vehicle but the crucial confidence of clear policy commitments at national, regional and local levels. A number of private-sector investors have already indicated an interest in making wider capital investment,[7] and some leading developers have considered in detail how this might be delivered. However, it is vital that investors recognise and buy into the ethos of garden cities. This requires long-term, patient investment that essentially trades lower returns for lower risks.

The public sector must play a leading role in the creation of political will, in the designation of a development corporation and in enabling the provision of public goods such as homes for social rent. But there is a real opportunity to attract large-scale, institutional, patient funds into a new generation of garden cities.

It has been suggested that new garden cities could be financed by private-sector investment alone. The Wolfson Economics Prize MMXIV[8] competition entries indicated that private finance could be the source of the critical up-front investment necessary to secure growth in the period before income streams from new development are secured (Case Study 9.03). This has been suggested as a way of reducing the need for public investment. The balance between these two forms of investment remains an area of controversy. An infrastructure investment bank that is backed by the government and can offer cheap, long-term finance for development projects has been proposed as one way solving this problem. Significantly, the willingness to invest in larger strategic schemes is dependent on the certainty that a delivery body such as a development corporation creates. This relationship between a state agency with the power to deliver certainty and patient private investment is crucial. This trade-off between lower returns and investment security could provide for a new era of private-sector investment in place-making.

Seizing the opportunity overall – as the Dutch developers Vathorst clearly have (Case Study 9.04) – the creation of new garden cities presents a long-term financial opportunity. Such development is not a drag on the taxpayer but rather, when delivered with imagination, can produce self-financing places over the long term. This requires, above all, a long-term vision, the right delivery vehicle and patient investors from both public and private sectors. ◆

Fig 9.05
An artist's impression
of Wei Yang & Partners'
and Peter Freeman's
garden city.

▶ CASE STUDY 9.03

HOW TO FINANCE A NEW GARDEN CITY USING PRIVATE INVESTMENT

A financial model for a new garden city offering 10,000 homes (30% affordable) and 10,000 jobs has been developed in Wei Yang & Partners' and Peter Freeman's Wolfson Economics Prize submission.[9] The assumption is that the garden city would be developed over 15 years, with construction starting in Year Four. Completions of private and social housing would peak at 1,200 homes per annum. Long-term institutional capital will provide project finance for a joint-venture delivery vehicle to support garden cities at reasonable cost.

The financial model demonstrates that the receipts from the disposal of land for new private housing meet all the costs of land acquisition; compensation for loss of amenity; parks and leisure; road, cycle and pedestrian networks; utilities; schools; and all other community facilities. Land for affordable housing is to be provided at no cost, and land for industrial and all business uses will not generate a capital receipt.

It is estimated that the total value of all the buildings in the garden city will be £3.09bn, in a location within 90 minutes of central London. All physical and social infrastructure will cost some £342m (excluding fees), and the joint venture would receive an average of £80,000 a plot for 7,000 private-housing plots.

On the basis of a real increase in value of 0.5%, inflation at 2.5% and a cautious phasing programme, it is estimated that the joint venture delivery vehicle will earn an Internal Rate of Return (IRR) of some 12.48% over 15 years, or an absolute cash return of £162m. These financial returns are available for sharing among the master developer (and their institutional investor), the local authorities, landowners, the CLT (for investment in the garden city) and the government (for investment in regeneration elsewhere).

▶ **CASE STUDY 9.04**

THE NETHERLANDS' INFRASTRUCTURE INVESTMENT MODEL

The Dutch have managed to increase their housing stock by 7.6% in 10 years in some 90 new settlements, using an infrastructure investment model. At Amersfoort near Utrecht in the Netherlands, a Joint Development Company was set up between the council, as one shareholder, and a consortium of five companies as the other. The private investors included those who had bought land in the area, but also those whom the city wanted to involve because of the good work they had done previously. The Vathorst Development Company (OBV) employs a small staff with a chief executive from the private sector and a chair appointed by the municipality. It works through developers and housebuilders, most of whom are members of the company, and through two social-housing companies. It is responsible for:

▶ land acquisition;

▶ urban planning;

▶ engineering;

▶ commissioning infrastructure; and

▶ allocating sites.

On the basis of the business plan for development of infrastructure and disposals, the company borrowed €750m from the Dutch municipal bank, Bank Nermeenten (BNG), which is the largest financial body in the Netherlands after the state, at relatively low rates of interest (5%) to be repaid over 15 years. These borrowings are repaid out of the proceeds from land sales, and the company has built up a 'buffer' that allows it to act entrepreneurially – for example, it funded the railway company to open a station several years before the population levels justified it, and it underwrote an entrepreneur to open a restaurant.[10]

Fig 9.06
Bathorst in Amersfoort.

chapter 10

LONG-TERM STEWARDSHIP

Community assets such as parks, community centres and public transport are vital elements of high-quality, attractive places, but management arrangements and long-term funding to maintain them are often considered only as afterthoughts to new developments. The garden city movement built on a long and rich history of community rights, ownership and asset management in the UK (see Chapter 1), and today Letchworth remains a great example of how long-term stewardship can work (Fig 10.01). Given the financial pressure on local-authority budgets, community-stewardship approaches to managing facilities are now more relevant than ever, and present an opportunity to put people at the heart of creating better places.

This chapter explains how imaginative approaches to funding and management can empower local communities to take control of, or have a say in, the running of local assets.[1]

What is Long-term Stewardship?

Long-term stewardship of an asset simply means ensuring that it is properly looked after in perpetuity. Under the garden city principles, stewardship is undertaken for the benefit of the community. There are many ways to achieve this depending on the place; the team delivering the development; and, most importantly, the residents of the new community. The garden city idea was predicated on a financial and governance model that meant that the community shared in the profits of development and had a long-term stake in the town's future through a system of participative democracy.

Fig 10.01
Letchworth Garden City Heritage
Foundation demonstrates the
effectiveness of good stewardship,
investing in everything from
healthcare services to art and
cultural events.

Once a new development is completed,
it is usually handed over to the local
authority for long-term management and
maintenance. However, the community
assets might be entrusted to a stewardship
body such as a local trust or charity.
Alternatively, the organisation that created
the development (a CLT, for example) may
continue to manage it.[2]

Who Benefits?

Long-term community stewardship of local
assets can benefit councils, developers and
local communities alike. Councils know that
new facilities will not be sustainable without
well-organised management structures
supported by consistent revenue streams.
Planning how assets will be managed and
funded from the outset (ie before they
are built) will reassure local authorities
that they will not be asked to take on the
maintenance of unaffordable assets. In
some cases, such as those of locally owned
energy companies, the council may find
that a new facility generates a significant
and useful profit.

Fig 10.02
Early creation of community facilities can help to create a sense of place and mitigate the fact that early residents are living on a building site; at Brooklands in Milton Keynes, some early residents cited the park as one such attraction.

Plans for sustainable community-asset management can also help the private sector play its vital role in building confidence and creating the positive vision central to the long-term success of a community. A new development will be more attractive to potential residents and investors if community assets are established in the early phases of building, and if intentions for their long-term management are clear from the outset.

New developments are usually built in places where there are already some residents. These people may object to the new development because they think it will undermine their own amenity. However, if it is made clear that the development will include community assets from which they might also benefit – new parks, arts centres, health facilities – and that rather than putting a strain on existing resources these new facilities will have a secure source of funding, they may take a more positive view of the development (Fig 10.02).

Building on the rights and powers set out in the Localism Act 2011, the process of engaging existing residents in the creation of a new community should include consideration of existing local assets and initiatives. It is likely that there will be existing local groups or organisations that could be involved.

Who Should Take on a Stewardship Role?

Most community assets, services and the public realm could be managed by a stewardship body. Certain services and assets will already be run by the local authority; the role of a stewardship body that has evolved through the development process is to add value for the community, by managing assets and providing services which supplement those already provided by the council. The stewardship body might be completely independent of the authority, like Letchworth Garden City Heritage Foundation or a grassroots initiative such as Incredible Edible (Case Study 14.03, Chapter 14), or it might be an additional service provided by the local authority itself.

Stewardship bodies can take many forms (Box 10.01). Suitable arrangements will vary from place to place and will depend on their function, the assets that are to be managed and the types of finance arrangements needed. There may also be more than one stewardship body managing different assets or providing different services in a new community. The most appropriate model may also change over time, as the functions and activities of the stewardship body develop (and, for a new community, as it progresses through the stages of project delivery). Some may be legal entities in their own right (for example, community interest companies), while some (such as CLTs, development trusts and housing associations) can adopt a number of different legal forms depending on the activities that they are undertaking and what the organisation is aiming to achieve.

Box 10.01: Typical stewardship bodies

1. Management companies

2. Community Land Trusts (CLTs)

3. Development trusts

4. Community interest companies (CICs)

5. Industrial and provident societies

6. Cooperative societies

7. Housing associations or Registered Social Landlords (RSLs)

8. Energy service companies (ESCos)

9. Multi-utility services companies (MUSCos)

Management companies

These are probably the most commonly used form of stewardship body. They are companies set up to manage assets (land, property or facilities) as part of a development. Membership/ownership of them is very often extended to residents, who become members or shareholders depending on the constitution of the company. They are sometimes called community trusts or development trusts (see opposite). The extent of participation in the management and executive functions of the company depends on the terms under which the company is established – usually, ultimate control of assets and expenditure is not passed across to residents until the development is complete, with the developer holding 'golden shares' and weighted voting rights until that time.

▶ CASE STUDY 10.01

EAST LONDON COMMUNITY LAND TRUST – ST CLEMENTS FLAGSHIP

The redeveloped site of St Clement's Hospital in Bow, East London is the flagship project for the East London Community Land Trust (Fig 10.03). The ELCLT at St Clements is part of a scheme of 252 residential units, of which 182 will be private, 47 affordable-rented (owned by the trust), and 23 affordable shared-ownership units (to be operated by the Peabody Housing Association). Local residents are working with national housebuilder Galliford Try (Linden Homes) to help restore the historic, landmark hospital buildings and use them to pioneer the capital's first ever 'permanently affordable' homes. The freehold of the entire site will be retained by a new community foundation – the Ricardo Community Foundation – which will then use the ground rents it raises every year to reinvest money within the local area through charitable projects. The Ricardo Foundation's board will comprise an independent chair and equal representation from the head lessees (Galliford Try/London Homes, ELCLT and Peabody), from key stakeholders (from the local authorities and the local community) and from a community association representing local residents. The public areas, while owned by the foundation, will be run by a management board comprising the head lessees. ELCLT will sell its homes according to a 'resale formula' based on local incomes (rather than the market rate), and the principle that no one should have to spend more than one-third of their income on housing costs. This seven-step resale formula is set out on the ELCLT website.[3] ELCLT will also restrict the resale value of its homes; households wishing to live in a trust property must sign a contract agreeing that they may only sell the home at the rate determined by the ELCLT's affordability criteria. This ensures that the house price increases only in line with wages, rather than in relation to land values and the open market.

Fig 10.03a / 10.03b
East London Community Land Trust, the first urban CLT in England, sets prices based on a calculation of real local incomes to ensure that they are permanently affordable.

Community Land Trusts (CLTs)

These are 'non-profit, community-based organisations run by volunteers that develop housing, workspaces, community facilities or other assets that meet the needs of the community'. CLTs 'are owned and controlled by the community' and can make sure assets such as housing 'are made available at permanently affordable levels'.[4] They are legally defined (in the Housing and Regeneration Act 2008) but are not a legal entity in their own right, and so can adopt one of several legal forms. Recent examples of successful community land trusts include the East London Community Land Trust (Case Study 10.01).

Development trusts

Development trusts are 'community organisations created to enable sustainable development in their area. They use self-help, trading for social purpose, and ownership of buildings and land to bring about long-term social, economic and environmental benefits in their community'. They are similar to CLTs, but have no legal definition and can adopt a range of constitutional forms and business models. They have traditionally been used in the regeneration of an existing area rather than in the development of a new community. The long-standing Bournville Village Trust (Case Study 10.02) falls into this category, along with recent examples such as the Parks Trust, Milton Keynes (Case Study 10.03).

▶ **CASE STUDY 10.02**

BOURNVILLE VILLAGE TRUST AT LIGHTMOOR

Since 1900, Bournville Village Trust has successfully managed and developed Bournville Village, recognised nationally as an exceptional example of an early garden suburb.

Today, Bournville Village Trust is using its experience to create a thriving new 21st-century garden village in Telford, modelled on Bournville, in partnership with the Homes and Communities Agency

(Fig 10.04). Lightmoor Village will feature 1,000 homes, including a quarter for affordable rent 'pepper-potted' across the development, once complete. As at Bournville itself, a strong emphasis is placed on providing the infrastructure needed to promote health and wellbeing and create a flourishing, mixed community. It has a school, shops, parks and a community centre – essential ingredients in

developing a sustainable and successful garden suburb. Dwellings must reach EcoHomes 'Excellent' standard, and all homes owned and managed by the trust will be built to Lifetime Homes standards.

The trust's commitment to community development and management sets it apart from others, and its stewardship model is the vehicle used to deliver this. The trust owns the land, and properties will be sold

freehold and leasehold with covenants in place. Covenants include a maintenance charge (that goes towards delivering community services as well as a 'wear and tear' fund), obligations to maintain the properties and a requirement to seek permission from the trust for certain alterations. Stewardship is a long-term commitment to the management and maintenance of a place, to ensure it continues to flourish in 100 years' time and beyond. It forms an integral part of how Lightmoor is managed, and characteristics of the model include a design guide to control building alterations, a commitment to public and open space, and resident involvement and empowerment in decision-making – including through the Lightmoor Village Estate Management Committee. In 2015, the trust held over 100 community events, and it plants a tree in the community orchard every time a child is born in the village – a nod to George Cadbury's original initiative at Bournville, where every garden was provided with a fruit tree.

Fig 10.04
Bournville Village Trust development at Lightmoor.

▶ CASE STUDY 10.03

THE PARKS TRUST, MILTON KEYNES

The Parks Trust is an independent charity that owns and cares for many of Milton Keynes' parks and green spaces, amounting to just over 2,000 hectares of river valleys, woodlands, lakesides, parks and landscaped areas alongside its main roads – about 25% of the new city area (Fig 10.05).

In most places, parks are owned and managed by the local authority, but the Parks Trust was set up in 1992 to care for most of the city's green space and ensure that the green landscape would be managed and protected forever without having to compete for funds with other council priorities. The trust was endowed with a £20m property and investment portfolio, income from which pays for its work in nurturing and enhancing the landscape. It is self-financing, and generates the income needed to maintain the green estate from its investments and from operations and enterprises including farming, letting of paddocks, events, sale of timber and commercial-leisure activities. The trust has a responsibility to ensure that it is financially sustainable in the long term. It does this by generating regular and sustainable annual income in sufficient quantities to fund all the work it wants to do to maintain and enhance the green estate – and by building its asset base to a size that, in time, will allow it to invest in low-risk investments and reduce its exposure to any future economic downturns.

Fig 10.05
Milton Keynes Parks Trust employs a high-calibre team and has developed a robust long-term financial model.

Fig 10.06
The Combined Heat and
Power plant in central
Milton Keynes, provided
by Thameswey Central
Milton Keynes Ltd, part of
the Thameswey Group
(see case study 10.04)

not aiming to make profits for individuals but do not want the administrative or governance burden of taking on charitable status.

Industrial and provident societies

These are organisations conducting an industry, business or trade – either as a cooperative or for the benefit of the community. Letchworth Garden City Heritage Foundation is an example of this model.

Cooperative societies

These are run for the mutual benefit of their members, with any surplus income usually being reinvested in the organisation to provide better services and facilities. There are a number of different types of cooperative society, which vary according to their core activity (for example, housing, consumer or worker cooperatives) but which are all based on the same legal structure.

Housing associations or Registered Social Landlords (RSLs)

Some housing associations or RSLs provide services to communities beyond their role as social landlords. They might be contracted by a local authority to maintain its public realm or run community centres. They might, themselves, own these assets if they are facilities that they have built as part of their own housing developments.

Energy service companies (ESCos)

An ESCo is a commercial structure created specifically to produce, supply and manage the local delivery of decentralised energy to large, holistically planned developments. For example, an ESCo can be formed to support a regeneration area; a sizeable residential development; a single

Community Interest Companies (CICs)

CICs are a special type of limited company, which exist to benefit the community rather than private shareholders. They are set up to use their assets, income and profits for the benefit of the community that they are formed to serve, and must embrace special features such as an 'asset lock', which ensures that assets are retained within the company to support its activities or otherwise benefit the community. The CIC is particularly suitable for those who are commercial initiative, such as an office or manufacturing plant; or a hospital or multi-unit development of commercial offices or retail outlets.

Multi-utility services companies (MUSCos)

A MUSCo provides all the energy-related services of an ESCo, but also provides telecoms and/or water services for a site. As successful examples of such companies (such as Thameswey Energy – Case Study 10.04) show, this model allows councils to provide an accelerated programme of activities to meet sustainability and economic/development objectives that could not be achieved as successfully through the model of council service provision, and activities usually adopted by councils of this size and location.

Implementing Long-term Stewardship

Once the most appropriate form of stewardship body has been decided upon, the implementation of its aims must be carefully considered.

Planning for long-term stewardship

Lessons from existing stewardship bodies have demonstrated that the key to planning successfully for stewardship in a new community is to:

▶ start early: to secure the benefits of mechanisms such as s106 agreements and the Community Infrastructure Levy (CIL), stewardship should be a consideration from the earliest stages;

▶ integrate with ongoing engagement processes: engagement around the development with local people and adjacent councils should discuss

stewardship at an early stage – including understanding how the development can facilitate or complement existing local initiatives, what local funding priorities might be and gauging the appetite for community involvement in stewardship structures and bodies; and

▶ think strategically and long term: stewardship considerations should extend to the broadest range of facilities and services in a new development, and allow for stewardship needs to evolve over time as the new community develops.

Paying for long-term stewardship

There is a range of tried-and-tested ways of successfully funding and managing community assets for the long term – including generating income by trading goods or services or from property portfolios, or securing income from charitable grants or through the financial incentives attached to the new package of community rights introduced through the Localism Act 2011. However, a long-term revenue stream is much harder to secure than up-front capital funding. Successful funding of stewardship must include:

▶ proactive and profitable management of land and property endowments: increases in land and property values over time can furnish a broad and reliable portfolio for investment, providing resilience and flexibility; there is an opportunity to be creative and entrepreneurial in generating income; and

▶ saving money through good design: energy-efficient buildings are cheaper to run and community buildings can be designed to have multiple uses; for instance, a well-designed facility could operate as a nursery, an art gallery, or a community cinema – or all three at once.

Running a stewardship body

When it comes to running a stewardship body, it is essential to have in place a representative and democratic governance structure; a body with the right financial, delivery and engagement skills; and ongoing and meaningful dialogue with local people. ◆

▶ **CASE STUDY 10.04**

WOKING COUNCIL-ENERGY ENTREPRENEURS

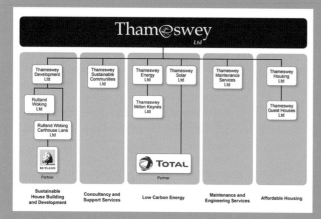

Building on the exemplary models found in Germany and Scandinavia, in 1999 Woking Borough Council set up Thameswey Ltd (TL), a private special-purpose vehicle formed through cross-party collaboration and agreements, initially to provide low-carbon energy within (and generate profit for) the borough, and subsequently to pursue a wider range of sustainable development objectives through its own commercial activities and joint ventures.

This included forming as an energy and environmental services company (EESCo) in 2000; in the same year, it completed its community-scale district-energy scheme, comprising a network of heat, cooling and private-wire electricity services for public, private and commercial customers in Woking town centre.

In 2005, Thameswey Central Milton Keynes Ltd (TCMK) was set up as a subsidiary of TL to further Woking Council's carbon-mitigation objectives through investment in low-carbon energy infrastructure in Milton Keynes – including building and operating a series of energy stations to supply low-carbon heat and power to the phased redevelopment of Central Milton Keynes. TCMK now owns and operates assets valued at £25m and supplies low-carbon heat and power to large commercial customers – including the headquarters of National Rail, a 10,000m^2 Sainsbury's retail store, restaurants, shops and offices – and over 1,000 domestic customers.

Fig 10.07
Thameswey Energy.

chapter 11

DESIGN AND PLACE-MAKING

The design of our surroundings has a direct impact on our health, wellbeing, and quality of life. This means that those involved in place-making – the design and creation of those surroundings – have a responsibility to ensure that any new development will provide the best possible outcomes for the people that will live, work and play there.

The garden city approach to design provides an opportunity to create innovative, resilient and inclusive places that will stand the test of time. The large-scale place-making that it requires provides an opportunity to think holistically about how a place will work, and understand what mechanisms are needed to turn an ambitious vision into a real place. The term 'garden city' carries with it a responsibility and opportunity to create exemplary, world-class new communities.

Early garden cities were consciously designed to be beautiful places that would lift the spirits of those who lived there. But despite Britain's heritage of design leadership, its current 'default' approach to the design of many housing developments is far from innovative. The pioneering emphasis on design quality and wellbeing stands in stark contrast to the unimaginative types and poor-quality design that characterises many modern homes.

Too often, new developments are designed without any consideration of local character or vernacular – resorting to standard house types, and street layouts that encourage car use and constitute a placeless 'anywhereville'. This lack of innovation has fuelled negative perceptions of development in general, which in turn contributes to public resistance to many new developments. Improved design and place-making can help to rebuild trust in the development process, and create more resilient communities.

At present, it is up to local authorities to determine the policies and standards laying the foundations for good outcomes in new development. Sound planning decisions require strong policy on design and place-making, and people with the expertise to interpret plans and champion good design. This is becoming increasingly difficult as local authorities have to cut spending, and as the continued deregulation of planning – including the removal of many building standards and the extension of Permitted Development rights – further erodes opportunities for good place-making. Of course there are always good designers doing great things, but these are limited compared with the example of many other European nations.

Nevertheless, key garden city design concepts rooted in the past – such as the power of art and nature to improve health and wellbeing – are more relevant now than ever. These concepts are essential to help tackle contemporary challenges like planning for climate-resilient cities – for example, by providing multifunctional green infrastructure and reducing freight miles using locally grown food. Garden city principles like long-term stewardship – looking after and paying for community assets into the future – must be planned for at the earliest planning and design stages, not least because they affect the physical design and layout of new places.

This chapter sets out the challenge facing those involved in design and place-making, and explores some of the key considerations that should underpin the approach of anyone embarking on the complex but exciting task of designing a new garden city.

The Garden City Design Ethic

The original garden cities have strong design associations – from tree-lined streets to Arts and Crafts architecture, and this is an important factor in their enduring popularity.[1] However, as Part 1 of this book showed, these visual associations almost obscure a deeper philosophy rooted in the pursuit of beauty - through everything from cooperative working to connection with the natural world.

New garden cities may not look like Letchworth or Welwyn, but applying the design ethic behind these places is essential to realising the garden city principles today. The philosophy that should underpin the design approach to new garden cities falls into five key themes (Box 11.01).

Box 11.01: Key themes of the garden city design ethic

1. Innovation and imagination

2. Marrying town and country

3. Cooperation in design and place-making

4. Character, distinctiveness and harmony

5. Spacious and well-planned homes

Fig 11.01
The garden citry pioneers tried hard to make housing affordable without compromising on quality or detailing.

Fig 11.02
Homes in Letchworth – details like grouping homes and leaving spaces between buildings to give glimpses of garden beyond help to give a feeling of town and country united.

Innovation and imagination

Councils and decision-makers have a responsibility to demand the highest standards of design and place-making in new garden cities. The garden city principles provide a framework for this, but they are not a blueprint. Councils should challenge design and delivery teams to be innovative in their designs and use of materials – making use of the latest technologies and materials whilst being sensitive to the past, and to the existing character and vernacular. Underpinning the process should be an approach to design and delivery that echoes the sustainability objectives and collaborative spirit of the garden city movement.

For the garden city pioneers, high-quality design and innovation meant the principles of the Arts and Crafts tradition. Twenty-first-century garden city developers can still learn from this tradition – which include

sensitivity to the local built heritage, a commitment to human scale, an understanding of detail and craftsmanship (Fig 11.01), and a strong appreciation of the power of art and the natural environment to enhance people's wellbeing (Fig 11.02). The challenge is to create new places that channel the innovation of places like Letchworth and Welwyn into a 21st-century context.

Marrying town and country

The garden city pioneers recognised the importance of not only having access to the natural world but also ensuring that buildings should be 'ornaments to nature, not disfigurements of it'.[2] A defining characteristic of the original garden cities is their landscape setting of parks, open spaces, and homes with gardens – a multifunctional green-infrastructure network (Fig 11.03). The resulting 'leafy and green' character is an important reason for their enduring popularity, but it also offers a number of benefits in terms of sustainability and climate-change resilience – including moderating temperatures, mitigating flooding and surface water run-off, supporting biodiversity and promoting health and wellbeing. The developers of a new garden city must aim to enhance both heritage assets and their settings through the proposed development.

Cooperation in design and place-making

Cooperative approaches to design and delivery – from regular public meetings and incorporating generous space for community and arts facilities, to creating cooperative shops and building companies - were an important aspect of the original garden cities and new towns and should also be central to new ones. Active participation from local people in the design and delivery process not only helps to build positive support for a development (Fig 11.04), but can also lead to better outcomes. Local people should be encouraged to get involved in the planning and design of a new garden city as it develops. This should include existing residents as well as new ones as they move in – as part of an evolving design and delivery process that might last 20–30 years. Active involvement in shaping the future of a new garden city can help to develop social links between existing residents and the people who move there as it grows, bringing together a diverse group of people to help shape and create the new place. This will need to be encouraged and facilitated by local leaders.

Fig 11.03
Tree-lined streets, verges and gardens like these at Cowslip Hill in Letchworth provide climate resilience benefits as well as pleasant environments for residents.

Fig 11.04
At Derwenthorpe, York, local school children were invited to name the energy centre and local play and nature areas, and draw a poster about the site as a way of feeling involved in the development process.

▶ **CASE STUDY 11.01**

LANCASTER CO-HOUSING PROJECT

The Lancaster co-housing project is a certified Passivhaus/Code for Sustainable Homes Level 6 (carbon-neutral) and Lifetime Homes-compliant affordable community-housing scheme. This groundbreaking exemplary (car-free) owner-occupied eco-housing project has evolved through a participatory design process with the 41 individual householders and Eco Arc architects.

Fig 11.05
The Lancaster co-housing project.

Character distinctiveness and harmony

Creating a new garden city provides an opportunity to set a framework for design and place-making that is both sensitive to local character and creates distinctive neighbourhoods – as was the case for the original, historical examples. This means that a garden city designed for Cornwall will look and feel very different to one designed for Norfolk: both will reflect the particular materials, designs and landscape of their locality. Garden cities must be exemplars of high-quality design, applying the highest sustainability standards; innovative use of local and sustainable materials – new and old; and high-quality, imaginative architecture, making use of expert craftsmanship (Figs 11.06 and 11.07). They should have 'postcardability' – a distinctive and recognisable character with imaginative and varied architecture forming part of a collective and harmonious 'whole'.

Spacious and well-planned homes

Arguably the most 'ethical' of all the historical garden cities' design ethics was their mission to provide spacious and well-planned homes for everyone. After all, one of Unwin's most famous rallying cries was 'Nothing gained by overcrowding!', with which he took on the deficient layouts of traditional bye-law housing (Case Study 11.02: Figs 11.08 and 09).

New garden cities should boast dwellings that are designed to achieve the highest possible standards of contemporary building-fabric efficiency – by, for example, following Passivhaus[3] approaches (Case Study 11.01: Fig 11.05). All homes in new garden cities should have decent space standards, building on the RIBA recommendation[4] that national minimum space standards be embedded within the Building Regulations (which set the physical standards for housing design). Similarly, providing accessible and sustainable homes in new garden cities should not be merely an option. The London Plan, which, at the time of writing, is being updated to ensure compliance with the current government's standards framework, states that at least 90% of homes should meet Regulation M4 (2) – 'accessible and adaptable dwellings' – and that at least 10% of new housing should satisfy Regulation M4 (3): 'wheelchair user dwellings'. As a minimum, new garden cities should strive to meet this benchmark.

Urban-design Principles for New Garden Cities

While innovation in the design of new garden cities should be encouraged, they should also apply clear, basic urban-design principles (Box 11.02).

> *Box 11.02: Key garden city urban-design principles*
>
> 1. Ease of movement and connectivity
>
> 2. Walkable neighbourhoods
>
> 3. Diversity of housing and employment opportunities
>
> 4. Healthy and active communities
>
> 5. Multifunctional green infrastructure
>
> 6. A human scale
>
> 7. Designing for climate resilience

Fig 11.06a / 11.06b
At Horsted Park in Kent, detailing
in the brickwork helps create a
sense of place while new housing
typologies and arrangement
homes take their cue from the rural
vernacular of Kent's agricultural
buildings.

Fig 11.07a / 11.07b
The Clay Fields housing scheme
in Suffolk combines contemporary
design and sustainable construction
with low energy use and A1:T177
local materials – hemp and lime.

▶ CASE STUDY 11.02

'NOTHING GAINED BY OVERCROWDING!'

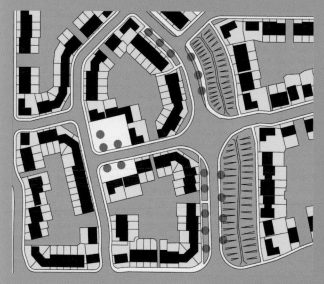

Fig 11.08a-d
Typical rear-court layout
of a common housing
development.

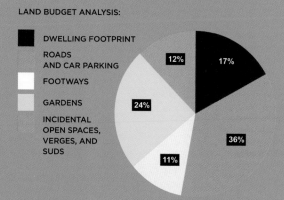

LAND BUDGET ANALYSIS:

- ■ DWELLING FOOTPRINT
- ROADS AND CAR PARKING
- □ FOOTWAYS
- GARDENS
- INCIDENTAL OPEN SPACES, VERGES, AND SUDS

12%
17%
24%
11%
36%

In 1912, Raymond Unwin published the tract *Nothing gained by overcrowding! How the garden city type of development may benefit both owner and occupier*, which argued, in some detail, that the traditional layout of bye-law housing was inherently inefficient – and that by turning the arrangement 'inside out', into blocks, the hard surfacing would be replaced by green space and healthier, and more pleasant, living environments.

In a TCPA centenary republication of the report, Patrick Clarke noted the contemporary relevance of this argument and compared the land-use budgets of common housing developments, with their rear parking courts, with a version of the superblock with green space on the outside (Figs 11.08 and 11.09). The comparison found that not only does this alternative arrangement achieve an apparently comparable density of development (and with more gardens and green space for residents) but that there were also significant cost savings on the construction of expensive roads and parking areas. And this is in addition to the climate-resilience and quality-of-life advantages of these proposals. This comparison highlights the benefits of thinking creatively about land use and amenity when considering housing layouts.

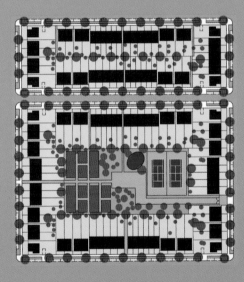

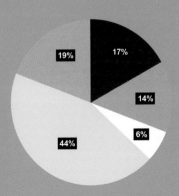

Fig 11.09a-c
Contemporary reinterpretation of the garden city approach.

Fig 11.10
In Vauban, Frieburg, Germany, a reliable network of trams, safe cycle routes, walkable neighbourhoods and car clubs have helped to encourage more sustainable movement patterns.

Fig 11.11
New garden cities should provide easily accessible work and a hierarchy of local centres.

Movement and connectivity

A good range of infrastructure is essential for new garden cities – not least, a transport network that makes walking, cycling and public transport the most attractive options; a range of community facilities operated and run by a community-led organisation; and a green-infrastructure network that makes full use of its functions (climate resilience, biodiversity, health, and social and cultural services). Its masterplan must integrate the garden city with strategic movement corridors and public-transport services, so that it is well connected to surrounding settlements and facilities (Fig 11.10).

Walkable neighbourhoods

New garden cities should provide a sustainable urban structure of walkable neighbourhoods, based around a network of mixed-use town and local centres in which residents can meet most of their day-to-day needs.

Diversity of housing and employment opportunities

New garden cities should meeting the full range of housing needs and aspirations through a diversity of housing opportunities, having particular regard to the needs of older people and the provision of plots for self/custom building (Fig 11.12). Homes in new garden cities must be accessible, flexible and sustainable in order to match demographic realities. There must be decent minimum space standards, applicable across all tenures. Self-/custom-build homes are an important part of the housing mix in new garden cities, and should be made affordable for people on middle and low incomes. Land should be designated for this purpose – potentially as serviced plots, an idea explored in Chapter 13. Homes should be designed for flexible working as well as bing located a sort distance from a range of employment opportunities and local facilities.

Fig 11.12
Self-build homes at Ashley
Vale, Bristol. Space should be
designated for this purpose in
new garden cities.

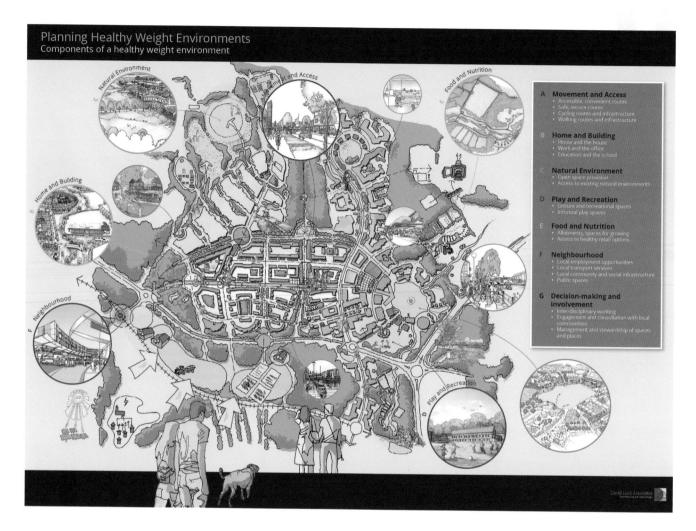

Planning Healthy Weight Environments
Components of a healthy weight environment

A **Movement and Access**
  • Accessible, convenient routes
  • Safe, secure routes
  • Cycling routes and infrastructure
  • Walking routes and infrastructure

B **Home and Building**
  • Home and the house
  • Work and the office
  • Education and the school

C **Natural Environment**
  • Open space provision
  • Access to existing natural environments

D **Play and Recreation**
  • Leisure and recreational spaces
  • Informal play spaces

E **Food and Nutrition**
  • Allotments, spaces for growing
  • Access to healthy retail options

F **Neighbourhood**
  • Local employment opportunities
  • Local transport services
  • Local community and social infrastructure
  • Public spaces

G **Decision-making and involvement**
  • Inter-disciplinary working
  • Engagement and consultation with local communities
  • Management and stewardship of spaces and places

Healthy and active communities

New garden cities should foster healthy and active communities by encouraging walking and cycling, and providing a comfortable, stimulating and therapeutic environment, bringing together the best of the urban and natural worlds (Fig 11.13). Provision of space for community activities and facilities, and a generous arts and cultural provision, as outlined in Chapter 14, is an important contribution to the health and wellbeing of communities and should be a consideration at the earliest stages of design.

Multifunctional green infrastructure

At least 50% of a new garden city's total surface area should be allocated to green infrastructure (of which, at least half should be public), consisting of a network of multi-functional, well-managed, high-quality open spaces linked to the wider countryside (Fig 11.14). This figure is ambitious, but includes 'non-green-space' green-infrastructure elements such as green roofs and green walls. Where it is not possible or desirable to provide a private garden with each home, dwellings should have easy access to shared or community gardens.

Fig 11.13
An illustration of the elements of a healthy-weight environment masterplan.

Fig 11.14
Letchworth retains an agricultural belt of land, which contains a 'greenway' route that circles the town, and also Standalone Farm – both owned by the Letchworth Garden City Heritage Foundation.

Fig 11.15
Higher-density Accordia, Cambridge – its shared gardens provide an opportunity for people to meet in the absence of private gardens.

A fundamental aspect of the historical garden city model is the provision of an agricultural belt to prevent sprawl and provide a local source of food and resources for the emerging market of the new garden city. The agricultural belt around a new garden city must be properly managed, with urban and rural land-management decision-making systems linked to ensure that it also provides for access for recreation, energy generation, agricultural production and habitat creation.

A human scale

A common misconception is that the garden city approach to development means low-density living. In fact, while buildings in new garden cities should be human scale a range of densities across different areas would be expected. Furthermore, lower housing density should not signal areas of higher wealth in new garden cities. The test is the extent to which the density applied allows for the realisation of the garden city principles: walkable neighbourhoods, access to sustainable public transport, etc. For example, in higher-density areas shared gardens provide an opportunity for people to meet and grow food where private gardens are not possible or desirable (Fig 11.15).

Fig 11.16
Low-carbon homes in
Letchworth Garden City.

Designing for climate resilience

Garden cities must be zero-carbon and energy-positive. Zero carbon means that, over a year, the net carbon dioxide emissions from all energy use within the buildings are zero or below; energy-positive, that they should produce more energy than they consume. Further information about climate-change resilience and creating energy-positive communities, including how this impacts design and masterplanning, is set out in Chapter 12.

Making it Happen – The Masterplan

One of the most important tools with which councils and delivery partners can meet the above ambitions is the masterplan. This provides the spatial framework for development, setting out the vision and establishing a basis for investment and delivery over many years. A new community is a 'vast tapestry'[5] that evolves over time; it is not built in one go. Experience shows that a strong vision of high quality and sustainability, within a framework capable of adapting as the community develops, is essential in delivering places that will stand the test of time, positively influence behaviour and promote healthy lifestyles (Fig 11.18). A strong masterplan results from an inclusive and imaginative process involving many stakeholders – one that can be both exciting and challenging. Masterplans today aren't the rigid blueprints of yesteryear. Contemporary masterplans are better thought of as frameworks that provide delivery bodies with enough certainty to direct infrastructure investment and development, but with the flexibility to allow for changing and evolving developments over time – the 'trellis on which the roses can grow where they will'.[6]

Each site presents its own set of challenges, opportunities and requirements – 'one size' decidedly does not 'fit all'. Chapter 8 sets out key locational criteria for a development site, including ensuring connectivity, an awareness of needs and requirements beyond the Local Plan boundary, and contributing to achieving sustainable development – all underpinned by a strong evidence base. The masterplanning stage requires further, and more, detailed evidence in order to underpin decisions on everything from the location of new roads to the number of community centres required. To get these decisions right from the outset,

▶ CASE STUDY 11.03

APPLYING GARDEN CITY DESIGN PRINCIPLES AT DERWENTHORPE

Fig 11.17
Derwenthorpe Phase 1.

Built in partnership by the Joseph Rowntree Housing Trust and David Wilson Homes, Derwenthorpe is a 540 home development on the outskirts of York. The development continues the theme of sustainable mixed communities which was one of the main drivers for the development of New Earswick, a garden village in York designed by Raymond Unwin and Barry Parker for Joseph Rowntree. At Derwenthorpe the properties are much larger than the average, feeding into Rowntree's original aim of everyone having a good quality home to live in regardless of their

wealth. Social housing is 'pepperpotted' throughout the development – meaning every street contains people with different financial opportunities. They are well insulated, so more affordable to heat, and benefit from large windows – maximising natural light and reducing the reliance on electricity. Each property has been designed with eco-friendly features including communal heating from a central biomass boiler and a drainage system that prevents flooding.

In 2013, Derwenthorpe won the Completed category in the Housing Design Awards.

The homes are surrounded by mature landscaping, including a large public pond and play areas. White painted brickwork and rubble walls echo the 'arts and crafts' style of nearby New Earswick. They include two-storey winter gardens which provide light, amenity and privacy. A connection to the Sustrans cycle route minimises the need for short car journeys.

Derwenthorpe has attracted a high proportion of residents who have one or more family members with a disability. The homes are proving to help provide a good environment for

people in a wide variety of circumstances. Each house is built to 'lifetime homes' standards, meaning they are easily and more cheaply adapted.

The Super Sustainable Centre (SSC) at Derwenthorpe supplies energy to surrounding homes and is additionally becoming part of the heart of the community, with regular resident events such as art classes, children's groups, yoga and coffee mornings making it a hub of social activity. Find out more at: http://www.jrht.org.uk/communities/derwenthorpe

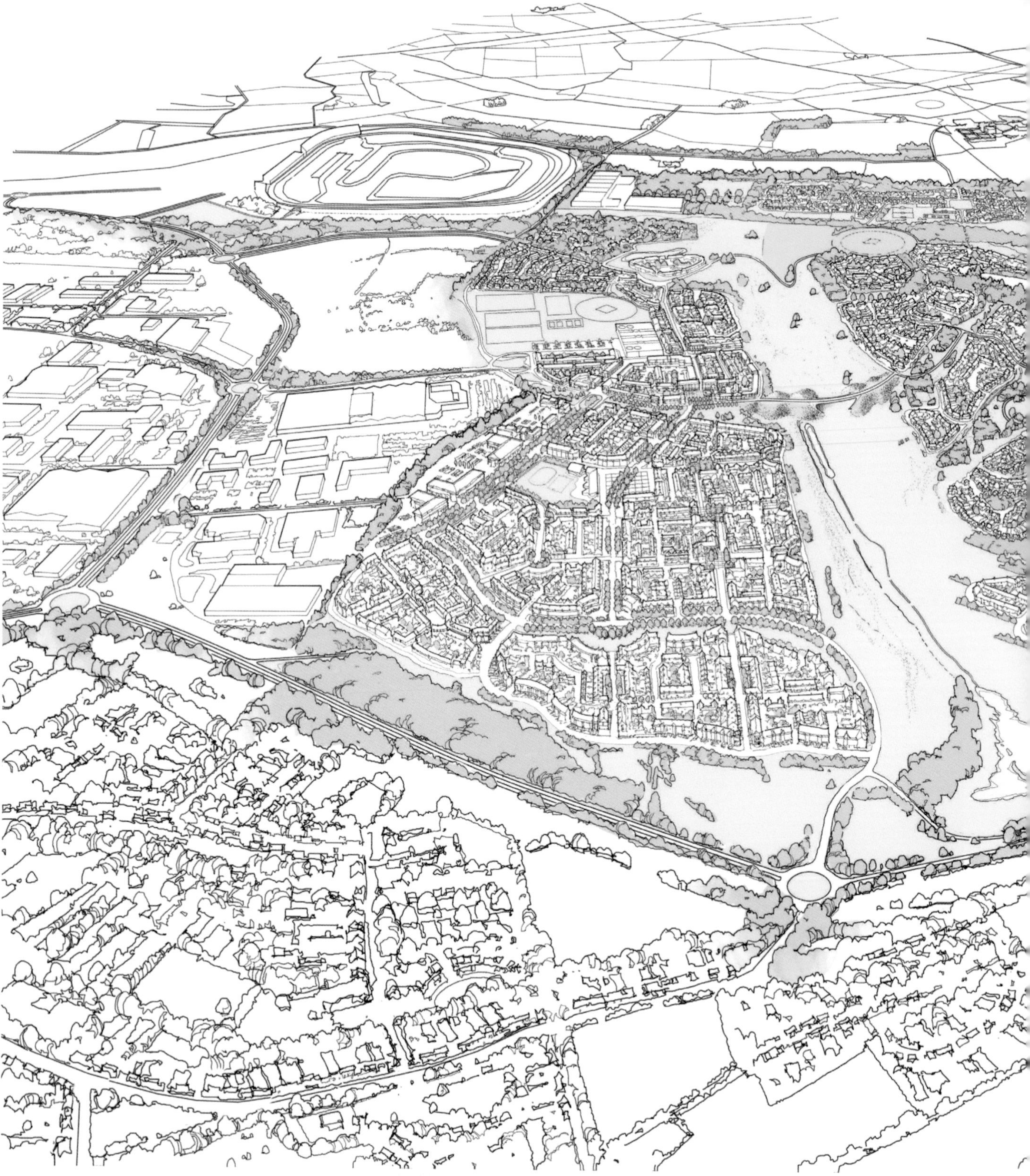

Fig 11.18
Priors Hall Park, Northamptonshire –
the power of a compelling diagram: a
masterplan provides an opportunity
to think holistically about how a
place will work.

masterplanning teams must have a sound understanding of the needs and requirements of the end users – those who will live and work in the new community.

Making it Happen – Good Design

One of the key challenges in creating new garden cities is how to maintain high design standards and principles throughout the long and challenging process of delivery. Too often, the reality of new development is a far cry from the beautiful illustrations presented at consultation events. The viability test, designed to ensure that developers are not burdened with onerous planning conditions and contributions that would slow down development (and affect profit margins), can result in a reduction in investment in design detailing and provision of facilities that contribute to the creation of well-designed and vibrant places. But there are ways for councils to encourage good design. Design codes have been a very popular way for councils to establish the design characteristics and standards that they want to see delivered in new developments. For years, consultants have been employed to create huge and detailed 'design code' documents, only for these to be watered down (or, in some cases, ignored completely) by developers. A more practical approach, employed successfully in some developments, is the role of town architect, including having someone physically on site during the build-out to have an overview of what is being delivered and ensure that high standards are maintained. Another strategy is to lay down a quality agreement for the whole development (Case Study 11.04).

An Opportunity to Offer Something Better

At the time of writing, local authorities and delivery partners face a challenging time for good design. Fragmented place-making policy, and the viability test's preference for minimal investment in the assets that contribute to good design, means that it falls to the most ambitious and innovative councils and delivery bodies to put in place the policy and mechanisms for good design. But there is also a huge opportunity to offer people a better option when it comes to new development – and harnessing the spirit in which the garden city pioneers created new places is a good place to start. ◆

Fig 11.19
Chilmington Green.

▶ **CASE STUDY 11.04**

QUALITY CHARTER FOR DEVELOPERS

At Ashford in Kent, the council has created a 'Quality Agreement' for its development at Chilmington Green. The agreement, which is believed to be a first in the UK, is a statement of intent, and sets out how the developer team will work with the council and the local community to design and deliver the development.[7]

chapter 12

CLIMATE CHANGE AND ENERGY

Garden cities are exemplars of sustainable living, and as such they must deal with the overwhelming challenge of climate change. It is hard to overemphasise how climate change affects every aspect of planning for new and renewed places, from overall location in terms of flood resilience to the detailed building-scale measures that can help secure urban cooling or the effective deployment of district heating. We are already feeling the effects of increased extreme-weather events and the impact that these can have on economies and societies (Fig 12.01). It is now inevitable that the Earth will continue to warm due to inertia in the climate system, and its temperature is very likely to increase by at least 2 degrees by century's end. Even if all the current pledges of individual nations materialised, levels of warming would be around 3 degrees[1] – well beyond what scientists believe is safe.

Planners and designers of new garden cities should work to the strong assumption that the most likely level of global warming at present is 3 degrees, and that the UK can expect sea-level to rise, higher temperatures and greater rainfall extremes.[2] Garden cities should also be designed to support the ambition of rapid carbon reduction by being both zero-carbon and energy positive (producing more energy than they consume) from the outset. This chapter explores some of the opportunities and mechanisms available for achieving this.

Fig 12.01
The 2016 floods in Carlisle, Cumbria, illustrated the power of increasingly severe weather driven by our changing climate.

Fig 12.02
Planning for large scale solar energy at Nine Elms, London.

The Garden City Opportunity

Planning for new communities creates an opportunity to address the complex challenges of climate change, both by reducing carbon emissions and by building in resilience to severe weather events. The masterplanning process creates opportunities to deliver renewable-energy systems (Fig 12.02), ensure energy efficiency in buildings, create sustainable transport systems and provide resilience measures. Above all, masterplanning can and must take the long view, considering not just the needs of today but the changing climate in 50–100 years' time.

Response to the multiple impacts of climate change needs to be embedded in design and delivery concepts from the very conception of a new community. This requires a strong understanding of both mitigation (reducing emissions) and adaptation (dealing with climate impacts). Reducing carbon emissions remains the key priority for our collective future, but decentralised and community-owned energy generation (perhaps based on a model familiar elsewhere in Europe) can also offer the opportunity of long-term income streams to help fund the wider place-making enterprise.

New garden cities must be 'beacons' of best practice in energy-efficient and renewable energy-generating developments – creating communities that are environmentally, socially and economically sound. They should be exemplar developments for effective approaches to the holistic provision of energy and other services, and they should draw from the latest advances in zero-carbon technologies for the generation, distribution and storage of renewable energy – as well as adopting decentralised and community-owned energy generation.

A major advantage of new garden cities is that zero-carbon and energy-positive solutions can be laid down across a whole town, permitting individual buildings to be incorporated into combined solutions rather than each being developed in isolation. This allows for the consideration of landform, layout, building orientation, massing and landscaping in order to minimise energy consumption. As new, linked settlements with a good range of associated facilities – schools, community and commercial buildings, and public and green spaces – garden cities provide the scope and scale to allow developers to convert innovation into cost-effective products, and, in the process, become market leaders in the zero-carbon housing market and energy-positive solutions. To achieve this goal, 'carbon awareness' – an understanding of the relationship between development

decisions, energy use and carbon emissions – should be embedded throughout the planning and design processes.

Do we have the political will to deal with climate change?

Of all the issues discussed in this book, climate change is easily the most challenging. This is not a technical problem, because almost every aspect of mitigation and adaptation now has well-developed technical solutions. It is primarily a political one, with apathy and outright hostility towards the idea of the climate threat. As a result, the current energy and planning-policy framework in the UK is fluid, with many policies changing and little short-term certainty. This applies both to spatial-planning policy and to the regulations and market mechanisms in wider energy policy. We are also currently out of step with many other nations who are moving quickly to deploy and support renewables. There is a growing gap between the global scientific consensus on carbon reduction and what, particularly, the British Government is doing in practice.

The government has made a range of recent announcements on energy and planning policy, which are of key importance for planning new places:

▶ a new national policy to create an effective moratorium on onshore wind turbines;

▶ the abandonment of the zero-carbon commitment for domestic buildings;

▶ the abandonment of the Code for Sustainable Homes; and

▶ reductions in the subsidies for renewable technologies.

▶ the strengthening of National Planning Policy Framework policy on climate change committed to in the 2017 Housing White Paper.

The UK Government scrapped the Zero Carbon Homes (ZCH) policy in summer 2015. However, the UK must still comply with the EU's Energy Performance of Buildings Directive,[3] which requires that by 2020 all new buildings in member states are 'nearly zero energy'. The UK's 2012 'National Plan' to meet this directive relied heavily upon the ZCH policy, as did our national planning policy. The recent decision of the UK to leave the EU has created even further uncertainty about which, if any, EU climate and energy targets the UK will comply with.

The financial viability of renewables

Despite this challenging policy environment, the long-term financial viability of renewables is very positive due to the declining installation cost for technologies such as photovoltaics (PVs). Individual commercial-viability assessments will be necessary to gauge the viability of differing sites, but garden cities offer the vital 'scale factor' that can reduce installation costs on, for example, comprehensive rooftop deployment and large, stand-alone renewable installations.

Key Considerations for Creating Climate-resilient Garden Cities

The overall corporate and design strategy of a garden city should consider four key areas in relation to carbon and energy (Box 12.01).

Box 12.01: Key considerations for climate-resilient garden cities

1. Zero-carbon status

2. Energy-positive status

3. Climate resilience

4. New models of energy ownership

Zero-carbon status

First, new garden cities must demonstrate the highest standards of innovation in zero-carbon technologies in order to reduce the impact of climate-change-inducing emissions. This means that over a year, the net carbon dioxide emissions from all energy uses within the garden city are zero or below. One successful zero-carbon development is North West Bicester (Case Study 12.01).

Energy-positive status

New garden cities must also be energy positive – aiming to produce more energy than they consume – by maximising opportunities for both energy efficiency and the use of renewable energy. The latter can be generated by a garden city stewardship body (as explored in Chapter 10, and outlined under the 'land value capture' garden city principle – Chapter 7) or by smaller-scale, community- and individually-owned facilities.

Climate resilience

New garden cities must be planned for climate resilience that reflects the long-term and complex impacts of climate change. This requires careful site selection and innovative design approaches. There is a close alignment between the wider principles of good design and building

▶ CASE STUDY 12.01

NORTH WEST BICESTER ECO-TOWN

Fig 12.03
North West Bicester Eco-Town
proposals – aerial overview.

Bicester is a market town in north Oxfordshire. It has grown substantially during the second half of the 20th century, and in 2009 North West Bicester (now known as Elmsbrook) was announced as one of four UK government-designated 'eco-towns'.

In 2014, Bicester was awarded 'garden town' status by the government. and is to receive funding to support the delivery of 13,000 homes. As part of this, North West Bicester Eco-town will be a sustainable new community of around 6,000 homes, with generous green spaces, community and social facilities, commercial premises and leisure facilities (Fig 12.03).

Its energy objectives are defined by its eco-town status and the policies set out in *Eco-Towns. A Supplement to Planning Policy Statement 1* – an ambitious government policy, regrettably revoked in March 2015 but with an exemption for North West Bicester. It remains the foundation for the new community's sustainable-energy objectives. Its underpinning ambition, as set out in the eco-towns policy document,[4] is for the new community to be zero-carbon.

SUPPLYING COMBINED HEAT AND POWER TO ALL HOMES

ENERGY CENTRE

POWER IS GIVEN BACK TO THE NATIONAL GRID

While national policy sets out the overarching sustainable-energy standards in the eco-towns policy document, the North West Bicester Masterplan gives the detail of how these standards will be met. A comprehensive 'Masterplan Energy Strategy' for the town highlights the importance of consultation and collaboration: 'arriving at the final energy strategy for NW Bicester has involved an iterative process of development and testing of proposals, discussions with Local Authority officers and consultation with wider stakeholders'. The first phase of the development is guided by four key energy principles:

1. **Onsite electricity generation** – every home has rooftop solar panels, making it the UK's largest domestic solar array (equivalent in area to two and a half football pitches).

2. **District heating/ Combined Heat and Power (CHP)** – a gas-fired CHP district-heating system will provide heating and hot water for every home.

3. **Energy-efficient homes** – the homes will be built sustainably, using timber frames, will be highly insulated and have triple glazing.

4. **Sustainable transport** – the community design will give priority to walking, cycling or taking the bus, with the aim of reducing the proportion of journeys made by car to 50%, down from the Bicester average of 67.5%.

To ensure that the masterplan is successful, it has been widely consulted upon within the local authority and the community. The North West Bicester Eco-town is setting out to be an 'exemplar', with the first phase of development demonstrating how a zero-carbon community can be delivered at scale. There is an integrated approached to achieving this goal, with energy specialists working closely with planners – and the Masterplan Energy Strategy is the key 'route map' for delivery.

in climate resilience – for example, the provision of green infrastructure, which can deliver urban cooling, gains for biodiversity and improvement to mental health.

New models of energy ownership

There is an increasing role for local authorities and communities in energy-supply ownership. Such an approach has many benefits:

▶ It generates income for local authorities to spend on services to benefit their local communities.

▶ It provides lower energy prices for local people.

▶ It generates local jobs and supports local businesses.

▶ It keeps money in the local economy rather than 'losing' it to multinational energy companies.

▶ It increases resilience through the diversification of energy sources.

The municipal-ownership model is widely applied in the EU (notably in Germany – Case Study 12.02), and some 60 UK local authorities have been exploring this route – including Derbyshire County Council (Case Study 12.03).

Steps for Developing a Renewable-energy Strategy

An energy strategy provides an essential tool for planning effective energy deployment in new garden cities by uniting energy planning with the wider endeavour of place-making. There is no perfect remit for such a strategy, but the 'golden thread' should be concern for all forms of energy consumption, generation, distribution and ownership. This means that issues such as building standards and transport fall into

▶ **CASE STUDY 12.02**

NEW MODELS OF ENERGY OWNERSHIP – HAMBURG

The north-German city of Hamburg, at the mouth of the Elbe river, illustrates the potential for mutualised energy-generation ownership (Fig 12.04). Its Wilhelmsburg district is Europe's largest river island, with a population of over 50,000 people. During 2006–13, Wilhelmsburg formed the project area for the International Building Exhibition (IBA) Hamburg, which has been a major driver for environmentally and socially sustainable regeneration projects within the area. The 'Renewable Wilhelmsburg Climate Protection Concept' set out a combined approach to sustainable energy across the district, with the overarching ambition of supplying the Elbe islands with 100% renewable energy. A range of measures have been implemented, including local renewable-energy production; energy-efficiency standards for new buildings, and for retrofitting existing ones; and CHP plants. A key focus of the Renewable Wilhelmsburg initiative was to ensure a high level of stakeholder engagement from politicians, civil servants in government agencies, local businesses and the community. Among the many projects already delivered are two initiatives that have helped to transform a pair of industrial sites – the Georgswerder Energy Hill and the Energy Bunker.

Fig 12.04
City of Hamburg masterplan for climate change resilience using decentralised energy systems.

Georgswerder Energy Hill

The 45-hectare Georgswerder Energy Hill is a former landfill site that for decades was 'off limits' for the residents of Hamburg. It was used as a dumping ground for rubble and domestic waste following the second world war, and was later used for toxic industrial waste. Today, the site has undergone a transformation. It is now an iconic visitor attraction (with over 60,000 visitors in 2013) and an important source of renewable energy, supplying around 4,000 households with electricity using wind and solar generation. Landfill-generated gas is also being utilised as a source of energy.

The Energy Bunker

A former air-raid bunker, built in 1943, has been renovated and converted into a renewable-energy power plant and 'heat reservoir'. The Energy Bunker provides enough heat for around 3,000 homes and electricity for around 1,000, through a biomethane-fired combined heat and power unit, a wood combustion system, and a solar thermal unit, as well as the waste heat from an industrial plant.

this remit even when their implications, like people's commuting patterns, can prove complex. Delivering energy-positive garden cities will also require strong political leadership embedded in the corporate strategy of the chosen delivery vehicle. The delivery team leading the development of the garden city will need to be prepared to set out the moral and scientific case for why a zero-carbon, energy-positive and climate-resilient development is needed. A strong communication strategy is vital in building public understanding and enthusiasm for new technologies.

The energy strategy should define the carbon-saving and energy-generation opportunities at each stage of the development process. This allows for strategic decision on technologies, such as district heating, which need to be installed during the early stages of a site's development. The preparation and refinement of the garden city energy

strategy should be completely integrated into the development process from the earliest planning stage and throughout the masterplanning and design stages. There is no template solution that can be applied to all cases, but each garden city energy strategy will need to consider four key steps to achieve the zero-carbon and energy-positive objective (Box 12.02).[5]

Box 12.02: Key steps to achieving the zero-carbon and energy-positive objective

1. Build the evidence

2. Consider technical choices

3. Choose the right energy option

4. Encourage wider community stewardship of assets

▶ **CASE STUDY 12.03**

NEW MODELS OF ENERGY OWNERSHIP – DERBYSHIRE

Inspired by the experience gained in Hamburg, Derbyshire County Council's ambition to cut carbon dioxide emissions and prepare the county for the effects of climate change is set out in its 'Climate Change Charter'. One of six priority areas addressed by the charter is the aim of securing local, renewable energy supply, which the council is seeking to deliver by cooperating with businesses, communities and partners to identify and make available potential sites for renewable-energy schemes. Already, six council-owned sites have been identified as suitable for ground-mounted solar installations; following consultation with local communities, the authority is now seeking planning permission for schemes on five of them. These schemes will be council-funded, with the revenue raised being used for the benefit of the local community.

Build the evidence

Developing an energy strategy requires strong data on the expected carbon performance of a new community, and the interaction of site design and energy use of its buildings and transport systems. This carbon profile provides the benchmark for future performance assessments, and allows for clear evaluation of the community's likely energy consumption and carbon emissions. It is then possible to assess potential energy generation by mapping the renewable-energy potential of existing and new heat sources. This should provide a comprehensive picture of the opportunities and constraints of energy deployment, and allow for the best choice of technologies for generation, distribution and storage.

Consider technical choices

There is a vast literature on the differing low-carbon and renewable technologies that can be deployed to supply a new garden city, and there is continuous and exciting innovation in this field – from the increased efficiency of PVs to more effective electricity storage.

In the same way, there is wide menu of innovative options on building fabric throughout the lifetime of a building. This incorporates its siting and design, construction, upkeep, use, renovation and eventual dismantling/destruction.

Choose the right energy option

Developing differing energy-delivery scenarios is a useful way of reaching judgments on the appropriateness of differing technologies for a particular site. These scenarios allow for a wider public debate on alternatives, and for integrating energy planning with the wider masterplanning of the site. Comprehensive assessments of the alternative scenarios are required in order to gauge their long-term effectiveness in carbon reduction and their financial viability. This is set within the context of the long-term community-ownership opportunities for energy deployment.

Encourage wider community stewardship of assets

Garden cities, as newly designed places, offer the perfect opportunity to lead the development of locally owned renewable-energy systems. Their energy strategies need to encourage and support community and/or municipality-owned energy. They can also encourage activity that promotes local generation, and link it to local supply and demand. Activities can include co-location of generation and consumption, promotion of smart-energy infrastructure and recognition of local energy supply as a tangible benefit. New garden cities can, and should, embrace community-owned energy systems, which provide long-term revenue, create jobs and safeguard fuel bills for householders and businesses. ◆

HOMES FOR ALL

New garden cities should be inclusive places meeting the needs of everyone in society. They must provide the opportunity for younger people to have an affordable home to bring up a family, and offer older generations the opportunity to comfortably 'downsize'. Garden cities must include genuinely affordable housing for essential, low-paid workers, whose employment underpins an economy on which we all depend. Garden cities must also deliver intermediate forms of tenure for people on average incomes trying to get on to the housing ladder.

This means that garden cities must provide a mix of tenures, including a decent proportion of homes available for social rent. Other forms of 'sub-market housing', such as shared-equity and low-cost or discounted ownership, should also be a component of the housing offer within the new garden city, with clear mechanisms to ensure this will be made available in perpetuity. Achieving genuinely affordable housing in new garden cities might seem challenging in the current economic climate, but it is made possible by the garden city model of land-value capture. Some up-front public-sector funding will be required, but the land-value-capture model makes genuinely affordable homes a viable prospect.

This chapter explores the opportunities available for delivering high-quality, mixed-tenure homes and housing types that are genuinely affordable for everyone in new garden cities. It begins by highlighting some of the challenges presented by the current policy and legislative environment, before going on to set out three overarching principles that will contribute to the successful delivery of vibrant, inclusive and sustainable housing.

Fig 13.01
Mixed tenure 'eco-homes' also
designed to Lifetime Homes
standards delivered by Joseph
Rowntree Housing Trust, New
Earswick, York.w

build and custom-build, and a programme
called 'Build to Rent', which aims to boost
the private rented sector, encouraging
institutional investment into the sector and
stimulating additional housing supply.

Homes available for rent will be an
important part of the housing mix in
newgarden cities, and the Build to Rent
Fund could support this.

Design and quality

'The Housing White paper has opened the
door to redrafting elements of the National
Planning Policy Framework (NPPF). As will
be seen below, the current NPPF policy
does not always ensure delivery of design
or build quality.

Recent changes to national policy and
building standards, combined with viability
test have made the provision of high quality
and well-designed homes event more
challenging.

The effect of the NPPF

The key policy forum assessing housing
need is the NPPF. All policy set out in it is
subject to a viability test, which is framed
to 'provide competitive returns to a willing
land owner and willing developer'.[3] The
viability test is challenging to the delivery
of high-quality, mixed-tenure homes,
leading to 'policy on a series of vital public
interest outcomes to be downgraded
or removed, particularly in relation to
affordable homes, building standards and
green infrastructure'.[4] This issue was also
highlighted by the House of Lords' Built
Environment Select Committee.[5]

Accessibility

Future housing must be accessible and
flexible if it is to match demographic
realities. The new technical standards
include optional standards similar to
those of Lifetime Homes and wheelchair-
accessible properties (Fig 13.01), but these
are subject to the viability test in the NPPF.

National Housing Policy

Although currently in a state of flux,
any coherent UK-wide housing
policy must address the twin issues
of affordability, and design and quality.

Affordability

During the course of writing this book UK
housing and planning policy was going
through a period of intense and rapid
change, with the passage of the Housing
and Planning Act 2016, Neighbourhood
Planning Bill 2017 and the Housing White
Paper in early 2017. Between 2010 and 2016
the political direction of travel has been
prioritisation of home ownership over all
other forms of tenure. Changes introduced
with the Housing and Planning Act 2016
include giving housing-association tenants
the same 'Right to Buy' their home as
council tenants have,[1] and a policy called
'Starter Homes', designed to provide first-
time buyers (under 40 years old) with a
discount on their first home, which in fact
is likely to price out 58% of the country's
'middle earners' and 98% of those on the
new 'national living wage'.[2]

The government is reviewing the
implementation of the Starter Homes
policy in the Housing White paper and are
taking a more balanced approach to tenure.
Perhaps more positively for new garden
cities, the government is supporting self-

The Housing White paper includes proposals around housing for our future population including welcome guidance for accessible homes for older and disabled people. There is widespread consensus as to both evidence of need and the cost saving to the wider economy of accessible homes. This is not specialist, 'niche' provision; it is well-designed, accessible and inclusive housing. As our population ages, the market for more adaptable and accessible homes will grow – and that will certainly be the case in any new garden cities.

Energy

Alongside planning policy, there have also been changes to housing standards with the new national technical standards published in 2015.[6] The new system replaces the Code for Sustainable Homes with additional, 'optional' building standards on water and access, and a nationally described space standard (referred to as 'the new national technical standards'). This means that there are no 'official' sustainability standards for homes in new garden cities. In addition, the government announced in July 2015 that it would not proceed with the zero-carbon allowance offsetting scheme, meaning an end to the zero-carbon homes policy. Both of these changes have significant effects on the ability to design 'homes for all', as efficient energy design is a key aspect of ensuring that future homes are resilient to climate change and affordable to heat and cool in the long term.

How to Achieve Homes for All

The garden city principles were founded on an understanding of the importance of decent homes in high-quality environments for everyone. Today, there is an opportunity for new garden cities to provide diverse housing-tenure options delivered by a range of providers, from development corporations through to smaller, citizen-led models such as cooperatives and Community Land Trusts (see Chapter 9 for further information about delivery vehicles). There is also a huge opportunity for self-build and custom-build homes to be part of the housing mix in new garden cities. Five overarching principles contribute to the successful delivery of a vibrant, inclusive and resilient housing offer in new garden cities (Box 13.01).

Box 13.01: Principles for vibrant, inclusive and resilient housing

1. Carry out a robust analysis of need

2. Set clear targets for non-market housing

3. Ensure a diverse housing mix

4. Deliver desirable homes fit for the future

5. Ensure that homes are accessible, flexible and resilient

Carry out a robust analysis of need

Garden cities built today must have a primary focus on providing homes for everyone in society, including those most in need. The nature of these needs will vary from place to place, and an up-to-date detailed analysis of not just local needs but the wider demographic, social and economic trends in a region will be required. This analysis should move beyond crude debates about 'affordability' to develop a detailed grasp of the kinds of homes and tenures that will meet the needs identified. Such data must be set within the wider, and vital, planning objective of socially mixed communities that reflect the diversity in age, household composition and ethnic background of modern Britain.

Set clear targets for non-market housing

Clear targets for social-rented homes and other forms of sub-market housing should be set for all garden cities. These targets should be dictated by local circumstances, revealed by analysis. However, we already know that the current housing crisis has locked out many people on low incomes. This implies a strong emphasis on meeting their needs, so, as a benchmark:

▶ new garden cities should aspire to 30% of homes available for social rent;

▶ other forms of sub-market housing, such as shared-equity and low-cost or discounted ownership, should form a further 30% of homes; and

▶ there should be a clear mechanism to ensure that such housing is made available in perpetuity.

This is a demanding standard, but, as the new towns demonstrated, it can be delivered if bodies such as development corporations are able to offer cheap land to social-rent providers. Between 69% (at Basildon) and 97% (at Peterlee) of housing in the Mark One new towns was for social rent – although it is worth noting that both these examples were large-scale, new developments.[7]

Ensure a diverse housing mix

New garden cities present a rare opportunity to provide a diverse range of housing types and tenures, delivered by a range of providers – from garden city development corporations or local-authority housing companies in partnerships with housing associations, private-sector housebuilders and Small and Medium-sized Enterprises (SMEs) through to smaller, citizen-led models such as cooperatives and Community Land Trusts (CLTs).

As highlighted in Chapter 8, the New Towns Act would need to be updated by the government to create new, modernised new town development corporations in order to ensure that they have sufficient democratic accountability at the local level and clear objectives to guarantee long-term place-making. One of the huge advantages of this approach is being able to control the build-out rate and ensure that a range of housing providers are on site at any one time.

Garden cities provide an opportunity to attract new entrants into housebuilding, by accessing the government's Build to Rent Fund, supporting SME housebuilders and encouraging a greater contribution from the wider construction industry.

Community co-housing

Community co-housing and CLTs are both models that could be adopted in garden cities today – certainly, neither are a new idea. Letchworth and Welwyn both included co-partnership housing models that provided a unique form of tenure combining features of a tenant cooperative with a limited-dividend company (see Chapter 2), whilst in continental Europe many such schemes have been developed in recent years (Fig 13.02). While co-housing is not yet mainstream in Britain, it is growing in popularity and success – as schemes such as Cannock Mill in Colchester demonstrate (Case Study 13.01).

At Welwyn Garden City, a section of the masterplan was given over to self-build plots, which provided some variation in design compared with the predominant designs of architect Louis de Soissons, who had been appointed architect for the town in 1920. Self-build plans were passed across De Soissons' desk, and consequently the final designs were not as varied as might have been expected – although Welwyn did achieve a consistency in its housing-design 'narrative'.

Fig 13.02
Vauban, a co-housing scheme
in Freiburg, Germany, where
younger families live alongside
elderly residents and offer
mutual support.

▶ **CASE STUDY 13.01**

COMMUNITY CO-HOUSING – CANNOCK MILL, COLCHESTER

This co-housing scheme at Colchester in Essex was granted planning consent in 2015 for 23 homes – a mixture of houses and flats (Fig 13.03). This sustainable community is based around three key sets of values:

1. **Good neighbourliness** – in supporting each other within the co-housing community and in making a positive contribution to the social, economic and cultural life of their locality – Old Heath, Colchester and the surrounding area.

2. **Active ageing** – as a way of encouraging participation, health, independence and environmental awareness.

3. **Eco awareness** – embodied in low-energy design, sharing of resources and integrated living arrangements.

The Cannock Mill scheme demonstrates strong support for high-quality design and sustainability:

We love the architectural and ecological quality of the designs and are confident that when built it will be a beacon for future developments. Our new buildings are designed to achieve Passivhaus standards for very high energy efficiency and very low running costs. They are designed to Lifetime Homes [standards] to provide accessible and adaptable homes for the future.

Fig 13.03 (a), (b) and (c)
Community co-housing project at Cannock Mill, Colchester.

▶ CASE STUDY 13.02

SELF-BUILD – HOMERUSKWARTIER DISTRICT, ALMERE, THE NETHERLANDS

Located to the south-west of Almere city centre, the Homeruskwartier district holds an innovative experiment in large-scale self-build, on a site occupying 100 hectares (Fig 13.04). It clearly demonstrates what is achievable by planning at scale: by early 2012, around 1,000 self-build homes had been completed; about 3,000 are planned in total. The local authority has masterplanned the area into a number of districts, each with around 720 self-build plots with different grades of building permit. All the infrastructure, including roads and utilities, has been installed by the local authority, which sells the plots at around £290/m². There is a mix of building types and costs, but on average three-bedroom homes cost around £150,000 (including the cost of land).

Fig 13.04
Self-build homes in the Homeruskwartier district of Almere, Netherlands.

Fig 13.05
Vathorst in the Netherlands, where social housing is designed to the same high standards as market housing.

Self-build and custom housing

Self- and custom-build homes should also be an important part of the housing mix in new garden cities, and land should be designated for this purpose – potentially as serviced plots. Self-build rates in the UK currently lag behind those in continental Europe, where the model is flourishing (Case Study 13.02). However, new garden cities provide a tremendous opportunity to develop these types of housing at scale in Britain.

Deliver desirable homes fit for the future

Large-scale development need not mean compromising on quality of design – as is clearly demonstrated in countries such as the Netherlands, where social-housing schemes have been designed to the same standard as market housing (Fig 13.05).

High-quality design is not just more desirable than the standard 'offer', but more durable too; the Arts and Crafts inspired architecture of Letchworth and Welwyn remains highly desirable over a century on – owing to the quality of materials as much as their design aesthetic (Fig 13.06).

Fig 13.06
High quality Arts and Crafts
social housing at Letchworth
Garden City, where 31% of
homes are socially rented.

However, applying garden city principles to new communities does not mean mimicking Arts and Crafts architecture. Instead, we should build on the design *principles* articulated by Unwin and Parker, who recognised the importance of beauty and usability as well as the need to build with the grain of the landscape, not against it. The right architectural style must be chosen for the particular site. Conformity to a small number of fixed housing designs, both externally and internally, should be avoided. Quality is key – along with the provision of the highest, sustainable building standards.

Ensure that homes are accessible, flexible and resilient

Homes in new garden cities must be accessible, flexible and sustainable if they are going to meet demographic realities. There must be decent minimum space standards, applicable across all tenures, and equivalent criteria to those of Lifetime Homes and wheelchair accessibility should be standard.

While there is no longer a mandatory set of government sustainability standards for new homes and communities, and policy support for energy efficiency and zero-carbon homes has been reduced, the creation of new garden cities provides a significant opportunity to develop low-carbon solutions at scale, as highlighted in Chapter 12.

A Call for Ambition and a Long-term View

Despite recent support for self-build and some co-housing models, the government's focus on home ownership and a lack of ambitious housing standards makes achieving 'homes for all' a challenge. But, backed by the right financial model and with a progressive local authority and delivery body, there is the opportunity to set high standards and meet the needs of both younger generations and the rapidly aging population. ◆

ART AND CULTURE

Successful places provide for the breadth of human experiences that make life worth living, and place-making must reflect all the complexity of human behaviours and aspirations. This means going beyond bricks and tarmac to offer access to the natural environment and vibrant recreational, artistic and cultural opportunities. It means being sensitive to people's emotional attachment to a sense of place as well as their economic needs. A vibrant social and cultural life cannot be imposed on people, but it can be enabled by offering the opportunities and spaces for them to enjoy the activities that define a thriving and creative place – everything from formal artistic opportunities to a broad retail experience. This chapter explores how to enable these opportunities in new garden cities.

Fig 14.01
Theatre in Welwyn Garden City.

'I'd Love to Live There!' – Why Art and Culture Matter

Culture distinguishes one place from another – it is often what makes one place more successful than another. The garden city pioneers placed great emphasis on the role of the arts and culture in improving wellbeing as part of a cooperative approach to society: in Welwyn, the first public building to open was the theatre (Fig 14.01).

There are many reasons why culture matters, particularly in new places. Its broad benefits range from facilitating physical and psychological health and wellbeing, contributing to economic success, creating place identity and attracting skilled workers and business, to providing support for education, skills and lifelong learning (Fig 14.02). Culture can also lead to stronger communities and provide welcome resources for existing residents, who thereby benefit from a new development from its earliest stages.[1]

Bringing people together

In the 1980s and 1990s, writers such as Colin Ward recognised the power of the arts, particularly music, to bring people together in new communities.[2] Art can celebrate and unite groups and individuals who represent the diverse ethnic, religious, gender- and sexuality-based strands of modern British society.

Fig 14.02
Driving regeneration through the 'making economy' – Building BloQs, a London-based social enterprise, has received Local Government Association (LGA) funding to create the biggest open-access studio space in the country.

Fig 14.03
Pride festival, Manchester – new garden cities should be places where great cultural diversity is celebrated.

Garden cities should be defined by this cultural diversity and vibrancy, with design contributing to everything from theatres to sociable neighbourhoods. This means shaping design with the needs and aspirations of everyone, from the playful child to the playful grandparent, in mind. Each generation produces cultures and subcultures that bind it together and help define its human experiences. Garden cities should provide the formal frameworks for this expression – through cinema, theatre and dance – but also leave open space for artistic dissent and 'chaos' (Fig 14.03).

Economic impact

Art does not just have a profound impact on peoples' wellbeing, it is also has a major economic impact on a place. Alongside a wealth of technical evidence to support this claim are impressive, practical examples – particularly in the realm of community regeneration. Philadelphia's 'secret garden' is a great example of how a project can provide multiple benefits (Case Study 14.01). This particular project both resisted an urban-motorway proposal and helped regenerate a whole neighbourhood by becoming an international visitor attraction.

Enabling the Arts and Culture to Thrive

The wider social agenda of the arts, and culture in particular, is central to the success of places. However, the multi-faceted – and sometimes unstructured, and even chaotic – nature of art and cultural needs means that they are often perceived as too challenging or expensive to incorporate into the planning process.

Reuniting art and planning

One particular challenge is the divide between the artistic and planning professions. Artists and planners, once united in a common endeavour, now rarely

▶ **CASE STUDY 14.01**

PHILADELPHIA'S MAGIC GARDENS

Philadelphia's Magic Gardens (PMG) is a visionary art environment, gallery and community-arts centre that preserves, interprets and provides access to Isaiah Zagar's unique mosaic-art environment and his public murals (Fig 14.04).[3] On one hand, it is simply the expression of a single artist, but, on the other, the installation has proved to be a cornerstone of the wider regeneration of the neighbourhood, bringing culture, business and people to an area in need of renewal.

Fig 14.04
Art and communtiy meet at the Philadelphia Magic Gardens, which has become an important focus for community life.

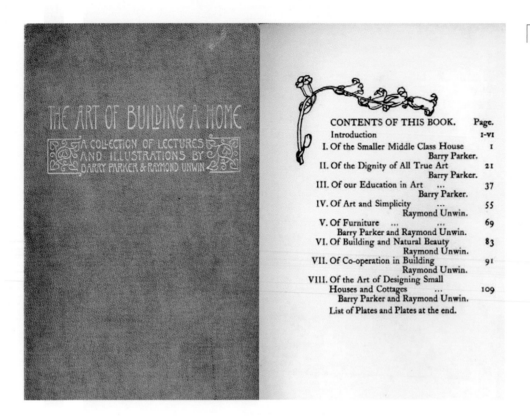

Fig 14.05
The design and layout of much new housing is a far cry from the principles set out by garden city pioneers Unwin and Parker in *The Art of Building a Home* which included three, lectures on the links between art and architecture.

meet and no longer share a common language (Fig 14.05). Planners often have the opportunity to engage with notions of how a place might 'feel' for its new residents, but don't on the basis that such ideas are too complex – involving, as they do, peoples' emotional responses to their environment. As the garden city pioneers recognised, the arts are far too often considered a peripheral afterthought or a bolt-on extra, which is often lost when a scheme's viability is considered. However, some developers have recognised the benefits of involving artists from the start of the development process (Case Study 14.02).

Stalin or Banksy: can culture ever be planned?

There is understandable anxiety about whether the arts and culture can somehow be planned in a rigid and formal way. In 1934, Stalin's Soviet Union notoriously imposed that country's new, compulsory Soviet Realist style; in early 21st-century Bristol and Hackney, anonymous graffiti artist 'Banksy' stencilled subversive mini-murals on public buildings – often falling foul of municipal authorities in the process. Part of the essence of art lies in how it evolves in order to colonise unexpected territory. Some of the best examples of how art has empowered and regenerated existing communities, often challenging formal planning processes, have been defined by their anarchic use of spaces (Fig 14.07).

▶ **CASE STUDY 14.02**

BRINGING LIFE TO NEW PLACES USING CULTURAL
HERITAGE – THE OLD VINYL FACTORY

Fig 14.07
Learning from Berlin's street art
scene, new communities need space
for creative chaos to avoid the bland
high streets of many towns today.

The Old Vinyl Factory in Hayes, west London shows how a creative approach to the use of space and strong private-sector commitment to the cultural and social life of a community can reap multiple benefits in regeneration projects (Fig 14.06). It also demonstrates how temporary buildings and structures might be used to host events as a site is developed, and to provide a sense of interest, activity and identity from the outset. Before building work had begun, the U and I Group (a regeneration and development partnership) commissioned a pop-up cafe and temporary museum, and invited musicians to record on the site. The strong narrative about the history and potential future of the site attracted new funding and partners such as the local university. These activities made the location a destination even before development was completed.[4]

Fig 14.06
Creating 'somewhere' from
'nowhere' - using the arts to
create life in new development
at the Old Vinyl Factory, Hayes.

The flowering of informal clubs and galleries in Berlin after the fall of the Wall was not planned, but it was enabled by the extraordinary availability of unused buildings and open space. Plans and strategies must be willing to take risks with the arts and culture, leaving space for innovation and responding sympathetically to new uses as they arise. The Incredible Edible project (Case Study 14.03), an initiative based on food that has been a major success, was driven by grassroots activism, facilitated by a council that knew when to 'let things happen' at local level.

Formal or informal?

Just as there are no fixed boundaries in defining art and culture, there is no easy separation between informal (eg local musicians forming a band) and formal (eg galleries and museums) artistic and culture activities. Both are equally important to place-making, and both require investment and support. Neither are there easy boundaries between the public and private sector because a vibrant cultural experience attracts people and business, which in turn adds to the attractiveness of a place. Institutions whose primary purpose is education can make a major contribution to place – for example, by drawing young people into town centres and by supporting the night-time economy.

Making it Happen

Place-making, and consideration of the 'physical' aspects of culture (such as museums, libraries, theatres, cinemas, galleries, archives, sports facilities and landscapes) should acknowledge, enhance and facilitate the development of culture's non-physical aspects (ie an area for a community's shared memory, experiences, identity, learning and creativity) as part of a wider framework of social sustainability (Fig 14.09).

▶ **CASE STUDY 14.03**

RADICAL COMMUNITY BUILDING IN ACTION – INCREDIBLE EDIBLE

In 2007, a group of like-minded individuals in the Yorkshire town of Todmorden decided to take action to improve their local community. They wanted to focus on something that everyone could relate to and take part in – and chose food growing (Fig 14.08). Starting with small herb gardens and community plots, Incredible Edible went on to back campaigns and support businesses; the group's activities led to the creation of learning centres, at the Incredible Aqua Garden and the Incredible Farm, and the emergence of the Incredible Edible network.

Remarkably, the initiative has been entirely community-led. In Todmorden, the group occupied public spaces (including council-maintained verges and brownfield sites) in food-growing interventions – sometimes without planning permission. Calderdale Council has since recognised the importance and benefits of the group's activities to the local community, and now supports the interventions. As well as simply staying 'out of the way', some authorities, such as Monmouthshire in south Wales (as well as Calderdale itself), have actively identified parts of the public realm than can be used for food growing and, through a simple and cheap licensing agreement, offered them up to communities for cultivation. Council community officers have also been tasked with building community awareness around these initiatives.

Fig 14.08
Incredible Edible, Todmorden, shows what is possible when people take control of their neighbourhood.

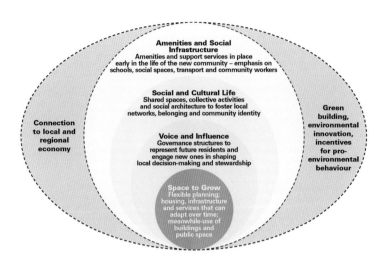

Amenities and Social Infrastructure
Amenities and support services in place early in the life of the new community – emphasis on schools, social spaces, transport and community workers

Social and Cultural Life
Shared spaces, collective activities and social architecture to foster local networks, belonging and community identity

Connection to local and regional economy

Voice and Influence
Governance structures to represent future residents and engage new ones in shaping local decision-making and stewardship

Green building, environmental innovation, incentives for pro-environmental behaviour

Space to Grow
Flexible planning; housing, infrastructure and services that can adapt over time; meanwhile-use of buildings and public space

Fig 14.09
A framework for creating socially sustainable new communities.

There is an absence of recent best practice for arts and culture provision in large-scale British development. This is partly because there have been relatively few such developments and partly because the arts and culture have not received the attention they deserve as key place-making components. Far from increasing arts and cultural facilities, austerity has led to many such institutions closing their doors or increasing their prices. In this context, Letchworth's story (Case Study 14.04) is remarkable.

However, just as there is no code for successful art, so there can be no simple blueprint for creating a vibrant cultural activity. Nonetheless, some recognised principles are vital for success (Box 14.01).[5]

Corporate and political leadership

The arts and culture can soon get lost in the development process unless there is clear political and corporate leadership. Successful 'place leadership' also requires a strong voice from communities and artists in shaping the ongoing delivery of a vibrant

Box 14.01: Art and culture – components for success

1. Corporate and political leadership

2. A strong local policy, and artistic and cultural strategy

3. Flexibility of design to meet changing needs

4. Securing long-term funding

5. Putting people at the heart of cultural development

cultural environment. While there can be no 'end state vision' for the artistic cultural development of place, good planning can create the conditions and opportunities for diverse artistic and cultural development over the long term. Place leadership involves vision, risk taking, playfulness, and a strong and inclusive dialogue with communities.

A strong local policy, and artistic and cultural strategy

There is a real danger that the provision of artistic and culture facilities can become a low-policy priority, or that they are viewed mechanistically in terms of 'how many' and 'how big' facilities might need to be. In fact, they need to be considered as an integral part of the design and delivery of place-making, and should be regarded as key policy priority from the beginning of the development process.

To achieve this outcome, new places require a strong strategy that sets the cultural and artistic narrative of place and offers a long-term programme of action, from masterplanning right through to audience development once the new community is established. The location, masterplanning and design of the detailed built environment should be seen as a holistic opportunity to reflect and embed art and culture. A successful strategy will need to include:

▸ a strong evidence base of the likely demand for artistic and cultural activities (eg advice from the government, local stakeholders and the wider sector);

▸ strong community participation as the community develops – to shape changing priorities and evolve a strong cultural narrative for place;

▸ close partnership with established arts and cultural organisations; and

▸ setting clear benchmark standards for the provision of cultural facilities, based on appropriate assessments; this can be a useful policy tool in negotiating with partners.

▸ **CASE STUDY 14.04**

INTEGRATING STEWARDSHIP AND THE ARTS AT LETCHWORTH

Letchworth Garden City Heritage Foundation is a self-funding charity that reinvests its profits for the long-term benefit of the local community, supplementing services and facilities provided by North Hertfordshire District Council. This includes the operation of a cinema (Fig 14.10), a day hospital for the local community and people who work in the town, a museum, a family farm, a community hub, a section of open space, a 'greenway' around the town, and other services. The fund is currently paying for the conversion of the cinema into space capable of taking larger, touring theatre productions.

The fund also supports an outdoor cinema and range of community-arts organisations and other cultural events, providing one of the most comprehensive arts and cultural offers for its size in England. The development of this programme was a positive response to a wider task of reinvigorating the town centre and promoting the night-time economy.[6]

Fig 14.10
Letchworth cinema was paid for through the recyled profits from the Garden City; it has also recently diversified, and, through its 'Live on Screen' programme, has the highest numbers of remote viewers of West End musicals outside London.

Flexibility of design to meet changing needs

A traditional approach to the provision of arts and cultural facilities was the creation of specialised buildings such as theatres or cinemas with a single fixed use. While there remains a case for such buildings, changing cultural aspirations mean that flexible spaces, capable of multiple uses and adaptability over the long term, are both more useful to the community and likely to be easier to sustain financially. This also reflects the changing nature of technology – for example, with live feeds of major theatre and music events being staged in cinemas and art centres. Letchworth's Broadway cinema currently has the highest viewing figures for regional remote showings of West End productions.

In the early stages of the establishment of new places, temporary uses should be considered so that arts and culture and can inhabit them from the beginning of the new community's life (Fig 14.11). Working in partnership with other sectors and stakeholders, there is also the longer-term opportunity to secure space for arts and culture through other forms of development (such as new schools provision), and to ensure that permanently affordable spaces are available throughout the life of the development (Fig 14.12).

Leaving informal external space for art ranges from installations like the Philadelphia Magic Garden (Case Study 14.01) to the provision of multifunctional green space for pop-up cinema and temporary festivals. Those delivering

Fig 14.11
Shuffle is a Community Arts Festival that has been created to form the basis for a 'Cultural Hub' in the mixed-use development of St Clements Hospital in Bow, East London.

Fig 14.12
Artists' studio at Hackney
Wick, London – culturally
successful places often have
a strong artistic community,
usually reliant on the
availability of cheap living and
working space.

new communities should maximise
opportunities for such 'meanwhile' uses
throughout the development process
– in partnership with the community.
In allocating space for informal cultural
activities, links should be made with
the provision of recreational space and
green infrastructure in order to identify
opportunities for multifunctional spaces.

Securing long-term funding

The construction, maintenance and
management of arts and cultural assets
require both capital investment and
long-term revenue. Artistic and cultural
provision must be seen as a part of the
infrastructure finance of any new garden city
development. The varying models of land-
value capture set out in Chapter 9 provide
an indication of the available options. Other
direct investment through grant aid from
government bodies or, more likely, charitable
trusts and funds dedicated to arts provision
could provide match funding (Case Study
14.05). Early engagement with both funders
and major arts and cultural institutions could
provide cost-effective opportunities for
establishing touring dates and temporary
exhibitions or, in the longer term, permanent
locations for parts of national collections not
usually on display.

Putting people at the heart of
cultural development

Garden cities are defined by strong and
ongoing community participation in all
aspects of place-making. Keeping people
involved and developing new audiences is
an open-ended task, and requires resources
and skilled staff. There is real danger
that arts institutions become elitist and
irrelevant without a strong guiding principle
of innovation and outreach to all parts of
the community. Strategies and provision
of art and cultural activities need robust
monitoring and review in order to reflect
the changing aspirations of the community
and new technology. ◆

▶ **CASE STUDY 14.05**

COLLABORATIVE ARTS AND CULTURE – MILTON KEYNES

The arts in Milton Keynes are integral to the new town's success and attractiveness as a place for people to live and work in, and to visit. The arts have been built into the fabric of Milton Keynes through the vision of its development corporation, which placed artists in communities, secured community buildings as arts venues and commissioned public art as development took place. Milton Keynes Council's 'Corporate Plan' sets out an aim of international recognition as 'World Class MK' through 'distinctive arts and heritage'.

Over the last five years, assisted by Arts Council England, Milton Keynes has significantly developed its cultural infrastructure. Invited by the Arts Council to submit ideas for investment, its two major arts organisations – The Stables and Milton Keynes Gallery – suggested piloting an arts festival; and Arts Council England brought potential partners together to make it happen. The Milton Keynes International Festival, held in 2010, featured 10 days of world-class arts events, reaching over 90,000 people (Fig 14.13). The event was held again in 2012 and 2014. In 2012, leading organisations and the council worked together, using London 2012 and the Cultural Olympiad as a focus, to put on hundreds of events in Milton Keynes' public spaces. A survey found that the 2012 'Summer of Culture' succeeded in changing perceptions of Milton Keynes as a place for arts and culture, and demonstrated the intrinsic social and economic impacts of its cultural offer; it generated jobs, developed local people's skills, created new opportunities and brought new spending into the local economy.[7]

Fig 14.13
Collaborative arts and culture – Milton Keynes International Festival.

Fig 15:01
Ebenezer Howard's ideas,
reimagined for the 21st century, offer
an opportunity to find a better way
to live.

CONCLUSION:
BUILDING THE FUTURE

There is no doubt that the garden cities concept offers solutions to many of the challenges that we currently face, from our housing crisis to climate change. This book has hopefully demonstrated the importance and practicality of creating very high-quality, inclusive places that can help meet housing needs in the UK, and housing challenges globally, over the very long term. None of the solutions in Part 2 are, of themselves novel, and in fact one striking feature about our collective future is the degree to which we have the technological solutions in our hands. The question is whether we will choose to use them?

Frederic Osborn, that great advocate of garden cities and new towns, was known as a 'practical idealist' – a phrase that encompasses the political ambition and realism of the movement. There is no doubt about the power of the idealism, something we have clearly lost in the current debate on the built environment in Britian, but the garden cities were, on balance, also real, practical successes. This is perhaps one of the most striking parts of the narrative of garden cities and new towns, which is surrounded by a kind mythological fog of failure. There were, of course, many problems, as there are in any great endeavour – but these need to be set against the scale of the achievement, like housing 2.8 million people in the UK's new towns, and in terms of how these problems originally arose.

For the new towns, some of these problems were unavoidable – like the availability of basic materials after the second world war. Some were about the dominant architectural styles of the time; some, like planning for the car, look outdated in the modern context of climate change and a concern for human wellbeing. Other lessons are less obvious, but reinforce the importance of the interlocking and holistic nature of garden city principles. The notion of community stewardship, for example, of mutualising assets for the long-term benefit of the community, which works so brilliantly at Letchworth, was one of the great missing elements of the later new towns programme. The centralised view of the new towns legislation, which gave much less focus to community ownership, allowed the assets of those towns to be comprehensively stripped by central government in the early 1980s and has left them, in some cases, without the cash for the renewal and development that could have transformed their ageing housing and public realm. Here is a clear example of why Ebenezer Howard's (Fig 15.01) vision of a different kind of development model is so important. It is vital, therefore, that we see the legacy of new towns not as series of unhelpful myths but as a rich set of lessons that can help us shape the future. Above all, we should recognise the achievements of the ambitious postwar generation, and reflect on why we seem incapable of even debating the future with any passion or commitment.

As this book goes to print, the UK Government has again returned to the ideas of new and expanded communities as way of dealing with poor housing delivery. Garden cities and garden city principles are now widely discussed. In this apparently supportive political context, one might be excused for thinking that the nation is set on a course for the 'sunlit uplands' of a sustainable future. In fact, the prospects for garden cities are much more equivocal nowadays – primarily because the gap between rhetoric and reality is widening. This is not a new problem; the 1920s and 1930s were dominated by housing developments that saw the 'garden cities' label as nothing more than a useful brand to sell more-or-less poor-quality suburbia.

The test of the new enthusiasm for garden cites is whether it genuinely does deliver, based upon the interlocking garden city principles and, in particular, on those critical elements around social justice and community stewardship. The opportunity and the risks are clear: we can build either genuine garden cities fit for the 21st century or 'urban extensions' with no homes available for social rent, no social infrastructure and no sharing of land values. The first course requires that the government sets clear standards in policy, and supports them with the right financial and legal structures. The government's commitment to updating the new towns legislation is an important first step towards this, but only if amendments go beyond local accountability to address land values and set a new creative ambition in design and delivery.

So where does this leave the garden city legacy? One could simply dismiss it as another name for 'good urbanism' or simply a milestone on the long journey of how planners and architects have sought to shape progressive outcomes. Are garden cities only relevant today as a historical curiosity? Indeed, this is now the orthodox view of Howard's legacy; however, it is both wrong and damaging because it places off limits those parts of the legacy that are most useful and most radical.

Significantly, garden cities were not simply a collection of design standards. They were a philosophy for a different kind of society: a sustainable one, built on the notions of equity and democracy. They distilled a wealth of utopian thinking about design, economics and governance. They recognised the power of nature and art in the wellbeing of people's lives, and joined those things through the medium of place-making. They were, as Chapter 2 set out, the culmination of centuries of argument and agitation about who controls and benefits from land. While for some, garden cities are no more than 'nice' suburbs with the odd tree, their future relevance lies in their ability to answer the question, how are going to live? Whether we like it or not, the UK will need to build new communities to meet the needs of its growing population and to deal with the extraordinary challenges of climate change. The question is whether we will meet these challenges with the ambition and principles to deliver places that the nation can be proud of.

The application of the garden city principles is, above all, a creative enterprise demanding both political will and the assembly of the best cross-disciplinary talent – from planners and ecologists to energy engineers and artists. At their very least, the principles offer a framework for good planning that has largely disappeared from British policy. At their greatest, they offer a foundation for innovation to construct communities that, like the original garden cities, offer a legacy of quality and inclusion for future generations.

However, in exploring the application of the principles there is a dominant message about the need for effective preparation and coordination. Garden cities will not be conjured out of the air by wishful thinking. Above all, they require the government to set out plainly how these new places will fit in Britain's wider economic, social and environmental development. This requires unprecedented cross-departmental coordination in everything from social-housing investment to energy deployment. Only with this kind of forethought and enabling will garden cities truly be able to deliver their outstanding benefits for future generations. ◆

REFERENCES

INTRODUCTION

1 See, for example, Philip Oldfield, 'UK scraps zero carbon homes plan', *Guardian*, 10 July 2015 <http://www.theguardian.com/environment/2015/jul/10/uk-scraps-zero-carbon-home-target>, 2015 (accessed 23 August 2016).

CHAPTER 1

1 P. Ackroyd, *The Life of Thomas More*, Vintage, London, 1998.

2 The name 'Diggers' was derived from the movement's occupation, and then cultivation by hand, of the land.

3 G. Winstanley, *Declaration from the poor oppressed People of England*, 1649.

4 Henry George was an American land reformer who pioneered land taxation, <http://www.henrygeorgefoundation.org>, n.d. (accessed 23 August 2016).

5 H. George, *Progress and Poverty: An Inquiry into the Cause of Industrial Depressions and of Increase of Want with Increase of Wealth: The Remedy*, Doubleday, Page & Co., Garden City, NY, 1879.

6 *ibid*.

7 F. Engels, *The Condition of the Working Class in England*, Otto Wigand, Leipzig, 1845. The English-language edition (authorised by Engels) was published in 1887 in New York, and in London in 1891.

8 *The People's Charter* called for universal suffrage for men, equal electoral districts, voting by secret ballot, abolition of property qualifications for MPs, and annual general elections.

9 W. Morris, *A Dream of John Ball*, originally published in serial format in the *Commonweal*, 13 November 1886 – 22 January 1887. It appeared in book form in 1888.

10 W. Morris, *News from Nowhere*, London, Penguin Classics, 1993 (originally published 1890).

11 P. Kropotkin, *Fields, Factories and Workshops*, London, Swann Sonnenschein & Co. Ltd, 1898.

12 E. Carpenter, *Towards Democracy*,The Labour Press, Manchester and London, 1883.

13 R. Unwin, *Nothing Gained by Overcrowding!* Westminster, PS King & Son, 1912; TCPA, *Nothing Gained by Overcrowding! A Centenary Celebration and Re-exploration of Raymond Unwin's Pamphlet – 'How the Garden City Type of Development May Benefit Both Owner and Occupier'*, London, TCPA, 2012.

14 E. Howard, *To-morrow: A peaceful path to real reform*, London, Swann Sonnenschein & Co. Ltd, 1898.

15 Formal definition adopted by the Garden Cities and Town Planning Association in 1919, and quoted by C.B. Purdom in C.B. Purdom, W.R. Lethaby, G.L Pepler, T.G. Chambers, R. Unwin and R.L. Reiss, *Town Theory and Practice*, Benn Brothers, London, 1921.

16 Howard, *To-morrow*, p. 140.

CHAPTER 2

1 The physical form of garden cities was itself an evolution of a long history of planned development, explained in C.B. Purdom. *The Garden City*, The Temple Press, Letchworth and J.M. Dent & Sons, London, 1913.

2 For a detailed description of architecture in the garden cities see: English Heritage, English Garden Cities: *An Introduction*, by Mervyn Miller, Swindon 2010.

3 The Public Health Act of 1875 required local authorities to implement building regulations, or bye-laws, which insisted that each house should be self-contained, with its own sanitation and water.

4 M. Hughes, ed. *The Letters of Lewis Mumford and Frederic J. Osborn: A transatlantic dialogue, 1938-1970*, Adams & Dart, Bath, 1971.

5 P. Hall and C. Ward, *Sociable Cities: The 21st-Century Reinvention of the Garden City*. Second edition, Abingdon, Routledge, 2014, p. 32.

6 *ibid*.

7 The International Garden Cities Institute is compiling a compendium of garden city inspired developments worldwide, <http://www.gardencitiesinstitute.com/resources>, n.d. (accessed 23 August 2016).

8 G. Allen, *A Hundred Years at the Global Spearhead – A century of IFHP 1913-2013*, for the International Federation of Housing and Planning, Narayana Press, Odder, Denmark, 2013.

9 The International Garden Cities Association now operates as the International Federation for Housing and Planning, with a focus on sustainable urbanism at all scales. There are still strong links between the two organisations, the TCPA representing IFHP in Britain.

10 Rosemary Wakeman's book *Practicing Utopia – an intellectual history of the New Towns Movement*, University of Chicago Press, 2016 provides a detailed exploration of the international exchange of ideas and political influences.

11 For a full description of the first-world-war impacts, as well as the role of art in planning and design in the early years of garden cities, see C.R. Ashbee, *Where the Great City Stands; a Study in the New Civics*, The Essex House Press, London, 1917.

12 For more on Letchworth's Scheme of Management see <http://www.letchworth.com/sites/default/files/attachments/scheme_of_management.pdf>, 2012 (accessed 23 August 2016).

13 TCPA, *New Towns and Garden Cities – Lessons for Tomorrow. Stage 1: An Introduction to the UK's New Towns and Garden Cities*, Town and Country Planning Association, London, 2014, p. 24.

14 TCPA, *New Towns and Garden Cities – Lessons for Tomorrow. Stage 2: Lessons for Delivering a New Generation of Garden Cities*, Town and Country Planning Association, London, 2015.

15 F. Osborn and A. Whittick, *The New Towns: The answer to Megalopolis*, Leonard Hill, London, 1963. One of the chapters is entitled 'Towns must have a stop'.

16 TCPA, *Best Practice in Urban Extensions and New Settlements: A report on emerging good practice*, Town and Country Planning Association, London, 2007, p. 38.

CHAPTER 3

1 A. Alexander, *Britain's New Towns: Garden Cities to Sustainable Communities*, Routledge, Abingdon, 2009, p. 24, cited in TCPA, *Lessons for Tomorrow. Stage 1*, p. 8.

2 In 1938, Neville Chamberlain assigned a royal commission, chaired by Sir Anderson Barlow, to explore issues around the concentration of homes and industry in Britain's inner cities. The commission's report concluded that large cites were a problem, and that it was necessary to plan for homes and jobs outside them.

3 P. Abercrombie, *The Greater London Plan*, London City Council, London, 1944.

4 The first London Plan had been published a year before, in 1939. Osborn had criticised this first plan as lacking the ambition for new settlements.

5 TCPA, *New Towns Act 2015?* Town and Country Planning Association, London, 2014, p. 5.

6 TCPA, *Lessons for Tomorrow. Stage 1*, p. 8.

7 L. Silkin, minister of town and country planning, introducing the second reading of the New Towns Bill, House of Commons Debates, 1946, Vol. 422, col. 1,091.

8 New Towns Act 1946 and 1981 – Chapter 68 (2) of the 1946 Act <http://www.legislation.gov.uk/ukpga/1946/68/pdfs/ukpga_19460068_en.pdf%20and%20Chapter%2064<http://www.legislation.gov.uk/ukpga/1946/68/pdfs/ukpga_19460068_en.pdf and Chapter 64, p3 of the 1981 Act http://www.legislation.gov.uk/ukpga/1946/68/pdfs/ukpga_19460068_en.pdf

9 Myers v Milton Keynes Development Corporation [1974] 2 All ER 1096. A legal ruling which meant that when land was valued for purchase by Milton Keynes Development Corporation, they could disregard the New Town scheme, but had to account for other potential uses that might be permitted on the site. From this point on valuation became even more complicated – and opportunities for land value capture decreased – as account has to be made for imaginary potential uses.

10 Lewis Silkin MP, New Towns Bill debate, 1946.

11 Alexander, *Britain's New Towns*, p. 74.

12 David Lock Associates, *Forward into the Past: Garden Cities*, David Lock Associates, Milton Keynes, 2014, p. 22.

13 See Alexander, *Britain's New Towns* for a more detailed analysis of the design characteristics and influences of the garden cities and new towns.

14 For more information, see: <http://www.nesltd.co.uk/sites/default/files/documents/EnergyWorld-handout-2011.pdf>, 2011, (accessed 25 August 2016).

15 Statistics from census data cited within 'The New Towns Record. Planning Exchange', *Idox Information Service*, <http://www.idoxgroup.com/knowledge-services/idox-information-service/the-new-towns-record.html>, n.d. (accessed 25 August 2016). Basildon has a population of 110,762, in 45,558 households according to the 2011 Census, and Peterlee a population of 26,633, in 11,462 households (see TCPA, 'Appendix. The New Towns: Five-Minute Fact Sheets', TCPA, *Lessons for Tomorrow. Stage 1*.

16 For example, see <http://www.talkingnewtowns.org.uk>, n.d. and <http://www.livingarchive.org.uk>, n.d. (both accessed 25 August 2016).

17 For more information, see TCPA, *New Towns Act 2015*, p. 15.

18 Memorandum NT 33, submitted by the Department for Transport, Local Government and the Regions to the House of Commons Transport, Local Government and the Regions Committee, April 2002. Published within House of Commons Communities and Local Government Committee, *New Towns: Follow-Up*. HC 889. Ninth Report of Session 2007-08. House of Commons Communities and Local Government Committee, TSO, London, 2008.

19 C. Ward, *New Town, Home Town: The Lessons of Experience*, Calouste Gulbenkian Foundation, London, 1993, p. 41.

20 L. Shostak, 'Here Comes Maggie' Milton Keynes Development Corporation referenced in T. Bendixon and J. Platt, Milton Keynes: Image and Reality, Grilford, Milton Keynes, 1992, p. 190.

21 Statistics from TCPA research. In 2014, the TCPA gathered data on the current state of the UK's garden cities and new towns, to understand what their current growth challenges are and how we might reflect on their development in order to inform the creation of future new towns – available as: TCPA, Lessons for Tomorrow: Stage 1.

22 Online surveys undertaken by the TCPA for research into lessons from the new towns, in ibid.

CHAPTER 4

1 S. Ward, 'Consortium Developments Ltd and the failure of "new country towns" in Mrs Thatcher's Britain', Planning Perspectives, 20, 2005, pp. 329-59, 331.

2 SPAN, publicity brochure for New Ash Green, 1967, <http://www.span-kent.co.uk/background.html>, n.d. (accessed 31 August 2016).

3 For an interesting account of the New Ash Green project and the experience of living there, see: J. Grindrod, Concretopia – a journey around the rebuilding of postwar Britain, Old Street Publishing, London, 2013, pp. 271–93.

4 Statistics from City Population, <http://www.citypopulation.de/php/uk-england-northeastengland.php?cityid=E35001362>, n.d. (accessed 31 August 2016).

5 Edward Milne (Blyth), question to House of Commons, 1 February 1968, <http://hansard.millbanksystems.com/commons/1968/feb/01/cramlington-new-town>, n.d. (accessed 31 August 2016).

6 T. Wordsworth and D. Crammam, Focus on Cramlington: 'New Town' enjoys new growth. Journal, 4 June 2014, <http://www.thejournal.co.uk/business/commercial-property/focus-cramlington-new-town-enjoys-7243968>, 2014 (accessed 31 August 2016).

7 TCPA, Best Practice in Urban Extensions and New Settlements – A report on emerging good practice, Town and Country Planning Association, London, 2007, pp. 27–31.

8 Ward, 'Consortium Developments Ltd', pp. 329–59.

9 Peter Hall and Colin Ward provide an overview of these attempts in Sociable Cities: The 21st-Century Reinvention of the Garden City. Second Edition, Abingdon, Routledge, 2014.

10 Government Office for the East of England, Regional Planning Guidance for East Anglia to 2016 (RPG6), TSO, London, November 2000.

11 TCPA, New Towns and Garden Cities – Lessons for Tomorrow: Stage 1: An Introduction to the UK's New Towns and Garden Cities, Town and Country Planning Association, London, 2014, p. 20.

12 Henry Cleary, who had responsibility for housing-growth programmes at the Department for Communities and Local Government 2001-11, provides a useful overview of the lessons from the growth areas and growth-point programme in H. Cleary, 'Large-scale housing growth – learning lessons from the last 15 years', Town and Country Planning, May 2015, pp. 222–6.

13 Kate Barker authored two reviews for the government. The Barker Review of Housing Supply published its final report on 17 March 2004, presenting recommendations to the UK Government for securing future housing needs. In December 2005, she was asked to conduct an independent review of land-use planning, and she reported on 5 December 2006.

14 H. Cleary, 'Garden Cities: What can we learn from eco-towns and growth points?', Planning, 10 February 2014.

15 DCLG, 'Homes for the future: more affordable, more sustainable', TSO, London, 2007, <http://webarchive.nationalarchives.gov.uk/20120919132719/www.communities.gov.uk/documents/housing/pdf/439986.pdf>, 2007 (accessed 31 August 2016).

16 DCLG, Planning Policy Statement – eco-towns: a supplement to Planning Policy Statement 1, Communities and Local Government Publications, London, 2009.

17 Summary adapted from Hall and Ward, Sociable Cities, second edition, pp. 179–80.

18 TCPA and D. Lock, Eco-towns: scoping report, Town and Country Planning Association, London, 2007, produced for the DCLG, p. 7. Though not involved prior to the launch of the programme, the TCPA was later invited to comment on the criteria for assessment of the projects, and to publish guidance and provide support to those places taking part in the programme.

19 Parliamentary briefing on the eco-towns, <www.parliament.uk/briefing-papers/SN04406.pdf>, 2011 (accessed 31 August 2016).

20 For more information, visit <http://communitiesgroup.org.uk>, n.d. (accessed 31 August 2016).

21 For a transcription of the process, see <http://www.publications.parliament.uk/pa/cm201314/cmhansrd/cm140124/wmstext/140124m0001.htm>, 2014 (accessed 31 August 2016).

CHAPTER 5

1 TCPA, New Towns and Garden Cities – Lessons for Tomorrow. Stage 1: An Introduction to the UK's New Towns and Garden Cities, Town and Country Planning Association, London, 2014, <http://www.tcpa.org.uk/data/files/Garden_Cities_/TCPA_NTGC_Study_Stage_1_Report_14_12_19.pdf>, 2014 (accessed 1 September 2016).

2 Statistics from census data cited within 'The New Towns Record. Planning Exchange', Idox Information Service, <http://www.idoxgroup.com/knowledge-services/idox-information-service/the-new-towns-record.html>, n.d. (accessed 25 August 2016).

3 Basildon has a population of 110,762, in 45,558 households, according to the 2011 Census; Peterlee has a population of 26,633, in 11,462 households. See TCPA, 'Appendix. The New Towns: Five-Minute Fact Sheets', Lessons for Tomorrow. Stage 1, <http://www.tcpa.org.uk/data/files/Garden_Cities_/TCPA_NTGC_Study_Stage_1_Fact_Sheets_15_01_20.pdf>, 2014 (accessed 25 August 2016).

4 www.gov.uk/government/statistical-data-sets/livetables-on-house-building - Table 209

5 GOV.UK, Live tables on rents, lettings and tenancies. Table 600: numbers of households on local authorities' housing waiting lists, by district, England, from 1997, < https://www.gov.uk/government/statistical-data-sets/live-tables-on-rents-lettings-and-tenancies>, 2016 (accessed 1 September 2016).

6 Shelter, 'Homeless households', Shelter website and DCLG homelessness statistics, Table 770, http://england.shelter.org.uk/campaigns_/why_we_campaign/housing_facts_and_figures/subsection?section=homeless_households>, n.d. (accessed 1 September 2016).

7 GOV.UK, Latest live tables on housebuilding (Latest update: 20/11/2014), <https://www.gov.uk/government/statistical-data-sets/live-tables-onhouse-building>, 2016 (accessed 1 September 2016).

8 www.gov.uk/government/statistical-data-sets/livetables-on-house-building - Table 209

9 N. McDonald and C. Whitehead, New estimates of housing requirements in England, 2012 to 2037, Town & Country Planning: Tomorrow Series Paper 17, Town and Country Planning Association, London, 2015.

10 RIBA, Over 50% of new build homes are too small for families, press release <https://www.architecture.com/RIBA/Contactus/NewsAndPress/PressReleases/2015/Over50ofnew-buildhomesaretoosmallforfamilies.aspx>, 2 December 2015 (accessed 1 September 2016).

11 Great Britain Ministry of Housing and Local Government, 'Homes for today and tomorrow', report of a subcommittee of the Central Housing Advisory Committee, HMSO, London, 1961.

12 University College London, 'Space standards: the benefits', report prepared by UCL for CABE (the Commission for Architecture and the Built Environment) in April 2010. Research conducted by Prof. Matthew Carmona, Prof. Nick Gallent and Reetuparna Sarkar, <http://webarchive.nationalarchives.gov.uk/20110118095356/http://www.cabe.org.uk/files/space-standards-the-benefits.pdf>, 2010 (accessed 1 September 2016).

13 W. Hurst, 'Agency brings back space standards', Building Design, 2 November 2007.

14 Design for London, London Housing Design Guide – Interim Edition, London: London Development Agency, <https://www.london.gov.uk/sites/default/files/interim_london_housing_design_guide.pdf>, 2010 (accessed 1 September 2016).

15 Department for Communities and Local Government, Technical housing standards – nationally described space standard, <https://www.gov.uk/government/publications/technical-housing-standards-nationally-described-space-standard>, 2015 (accessed 1 September 2016).

16 RIBA, '#HomeWise', Royal Institute of British Architects, London, https://www.architecture.com/RIBA/Campaigns%20and%20issues/Assets/Files/HomewiseReport2015.pdf, 2015 (accessed 1 September 2016).

17 ibid.

18 Simon Nicol, Mike Roys and Helen Garrett, The cost of poor housing to the NHS, BRE briefing paper, <https://www.bre.co.uk/filelibrary/pdf/87741-Cost-of-Poor-Housing-Briefing-Paper-v3.pdf>, 2015 (accessed 1 September 2016).

19 N. Macfadyen, Health and Garden Cities. A re-publication of the Garden Cities and Town Planning Association's 1938 pamphlet on the health benefits of garden cities. Town & Country Planning: Tomorrow Series Paper 14, Town and Country Planning Association, London, 2013.

20 A. Ross, 'Obesity: the role of planning', Planning, 31 October 2011, <www.planningresource.co.uk/Design/article/1101546/obesity-role-planning>, 2011 (accessed 1 September 2016) available on request from the TCPA.

21 LGA, Councils respond to public health grants allocation, press release, <http://www.local.gov.uk/web/guest/health-wellbeing-and-adult-social-care/-/journal_content/56/10180/7689913/NEWS#sthash.WcpaOELl.dpuf>, 11 February 2016 (accessed 1 September 2016).

REFERENCES

22 LGA, *Councils respond to ADPH report on impact of public health funding reductions*, press release, <http://www.local.gov.uk/web/guest/media-releases/-/journal_content/56/10180/7676769/NEWS#sthash.NB3dRq87.dpuf>, 3 February 2016 (accessed 1 September 2016).

23 NHS England, *Healthy New Towns*, 2015, <https://www.england.nhs.uk/ourwork/innovation/healthy-new-towns>, n.d. (accessed 1 September 2016).

24 www.england.nhs.uk/ourwork/innovation/healthy-new-towns/

25 *ibid.*

26 www.theccc.org.uk/wp-content/uploads/2015/11/Sectoral-scenarios-for-the-fifth-carbon-budget-Committee-on-Climate-Change.pdf (page 30)

CHAPTER 6

1 Department for Communities and Local Government, *National Planning Policy Framework, 2012. Paragraph 52*, < https://www.gov.uk/government/publications/national-planning-policy-framework--2, (accessed 26 September 2016).

2 TCPA garden city campaign documents are available at <http://www.tcpa.org.uk/pages/garden-cities.html accessed 4 October 2016).

3 For further details, see <http://www.policyexchange.org.uk/item/wolfson-economics-prize>, n.d. (accessed 1 September 2016).

4 BBC News, *Conservatives 'suppressing garden cities report'*, <http://www.bbc.co.uk/news/uk-politics-25694465>, 11 January 2014 (accessed 1 September 2016).

5 *Mobilising across the nation to build the homes our children need*, the Lyons Housing Review, <http://www.yourbritain.org.uk/uploads/editor/files/The_Lyons_Housing_Review_2.pdf>, 2014 (accessed 1 September 2016).

6 Department for Communities and Local Government, Locally-Led Garden Villages, Towns and Cities, <https://www.gov.uk/government/uploads/system/uploads/attachment_data/file/508205/Locally-led_garden_villages__towns_and_cities.pdf> March 2016 (accessed 23 September 2016). p. 4.

7 Conservative manifesto: https://s3-eu-west-1.amazonaws.com/manifesto2015/ConservativeManifesto2015.pdf

2016 budget report: https://www.gov.uk/government/uploads/system/uploads/attachment_data/file/508193/HMT_Budget_2016_Web_Accessible.pdf

Housing white paper 2017: https://www.gov.uk/government/collections/housing-white-paper

TCPA Joint statement: https://www.tcpa.org.uk/blog/house-white-paper-time-to-update-the-new-towns-act

8 Buglife are one organisation to make this case, <https://www.buglife.org.uk/campaigns-and-our-work/habitat-projects/brownfields>, n.d. (accessed 1 September 2016).

9 Homes and Communities Agency, March 2011. Previously developed land that may be available for development: Results from the 2009 National Land Use Database of Previously-Developed Land in England <http://www.homesandcommunities.co.uk/sites/default/files/our-work/nlud-report-2009.pdf> (accessed 23 September 2016).

10 A report on housing produced by the Tudor Walters Parliamentary Committee in November 1918. Its recommendations set the standards for council house design and location for the next 90 years.

11 Unwin, R. Town Planning in Practice: an introduction to the art of designing cities and suburbs, 1909, Longmans, Green & Co.London. p. 319-320.

12 Office for National Statistics, *Where do we Commute to?* Online resource: <www.neighbourhood.statistics.gov.uk/HTMLDocs/dvc193>, n.d. (accessed 1 September 2016).

13 Milton Keynes Council, *Note on Commuting to and from Milton Keynes*, Document Number: MKC/25, <www.milton-keynes.gov.uk/assets/attach/11658/MKC-25_REVISED_COMMUTING_PAPER-PE.pdf>, 2012 (accessed 1 September 2016).

14 Garden Cities Myth-Buster, a short guide to myths and truths about creating new garden cities, TCPA (2014) https://www.tcpa.org.uk/Handlers/Download.ashx?IDMF=5eb6b9b0-6374-41a8-b4ae-ba2a80937222

15 Letchworth Garden City Heritage Foundation, *Economic Assessment of Growth Options, Final Report*, 2013, by Nathaniel Litchfield and Partners for Letchworth Garden City Heritage Foundation.

CHAPTER 7

1 E. Howard, *Garden Cities of To-Morrow*, Swan Sonnenschein, London, 1902, p. 10.

2 Sport England supported by Public Health England, *Active Design – Planning for health and wellbeing through sport and physical activity*, Sport England, London, 2015, <https://www.sportengland.org/facilities-planning/planning-for-sport/planning-tools-and-guidance/active-design>, n.d. (accessed 2 September 2016)

3 *Biodiversity 2020: A strategy for England's wildlife and ecosystem services*, Department for Environment, Food and Rural Affairs, London, <https://www.gov.uk/government/uploads/system/uploads/attachment_data/file/69446/pb13583-biodiversity-strategy-2020-111111.pdf>, 2011 (accessed 2 September 2016).

4 This standard was one defined by an expert panel for use in the government's eco-towns programme and remains a useful benchmark for today.

CHAPTER 8

1 The duty to cooperate was created in the Localism Act 2011 and places a legal duty on local planning authorities, county councils in England and public bodies to engage 'constructively, actively and on an ongoing basis' to maximise the effectiveness of Local and Marine Plan preparation in the context of strategic cross boundary matters. The duty to cooperate is not a duty to agree.

2 Further details about the North Northamptonshire JPU can be found at <http://www.nnjpu.org.uk/default.asp>, 2016 (accessed 2 September 2016).

3 TCPA, *Best Practice in Urban Extensions and New Settlements – A report on emerging good practice*, Town and Country Planning Association, London, 2007, <http://www.tcpa.org.uk/data/files/nsue.pdf>, 2007 (accessed 2 September 2016).

4 *ibid.*

5 P. Hall and C. Ward, *Sociable Cities: The 21st-Century Reinvention of the Garden City*. Second edition, Abingdon, Routledge, 2014.

6 The TCPA explored some of the geographies that can contribute to rebalancing Britain, in *The Lie of the Land! England in the 21st* Century, summary report, Town and Country Planning Association, London, 2012.

7 These two routes reflect what is possible without an entirely new act of parliament. At the time of writing, an amended version of the National Strategic Infrastructure Project regime was also discussed as a possible route. This has not been included here as it would require new primary legislation – extremely unlikely in the current political climate.

8 See, for example, <http://www.tcpa.org.uk/pages/connecting-england-connecting-england-76.html>, n.d. (accessed 2 September 2016).

9 The TCPA has published a practical guide to locating and consenting new garden cities, which provides further detail of the approaches and criteria outlined in this chapter http://www.tcpa.org.uk/guidance-for-delivering-new-garden-cities (accessed November 2016)

CHAPTER 9

1 Compulsory purchase involves a public body forcing a private landowner to sell land that is required in the wider public interest. More information at <https://www.gov.uk/government/collections/compulsory-purchase-system-guidance>, n.d. (accessed 26 September 2016).

2 Betterment is an increase in land values that arises from the action of public authorities, such as providing infrastructure or granting planning permission.

3 Further information on this topic can be found in TCPA, *Putting Garden Cities at the Heart of the Housing and Planning Bill*, parliamentary briefing, <http://www.tcpa.org.uk/data/files/resources/1266/TCPA-Garden_Cities_Bill-Briefing-15-10-20.pdf>, 2015 (accessed 2 September 2016).

4 Viability assessments are required by national planning policy, and are designed to limit the scale of obligations and policy requirements placed on a developer in order that their ability to be developed viably is not threatened. Too often, they are used as an excuse to reduce key planning gains such as affordable housing, <http://planningguidance.communities.gov.uk/blog/guidance/viability-guidance>, 2015 (accessed 2 September 2016).

5 TCPA, *Land value capture and infrastructure delivery through SLICs*, Town & Country Planning: Tomorrow Series Paper 13, Town and Country Planning Association, London, <http://www.tcpa.org.uk/data/files/TomorrowSP_SLICs.pdf>, n.d. (accessed 2 September 2016).

6 Full details are set out in TCPA, *New Towns Act 2015?* Town and Country Planning Association, London, 2014.

7 These two routes reflect what is possible without an entirely new act of parliament. At the time of writing, an amended version of the National Strategic Infrastructure Project regime was also discussed as a possible route. This has not been included here as it would require new primary legislation – extremely unlikely in the current political climate.

8 8: See, for example, <http://www.tcpa.org.uk/pages/connecting-england-connecting-england-76.html>, n.d. (accessed 2 September 2016).

9 Wei Yang & Partners and Peter Freeman in collaboration with Buro Happold and Shared Intelligence with support from Gardiner & Theobald, *New Garden Cities: Visionary, Economically Viable and Popular: Wolfson Economics Prize 2014*, London, 2014.

10 N. Falk, Making Eco Towns Work: Developing Vathorst, Amersfoort NL, URBED, London, 2008, <http://urbed.coop/sites/default/files/Making%20Ecotowns%20work%20-%20developing%20Vathorst.pdf >, 2008 (accessed 26 September 2016).

CHAPTER 10

1   A recent TCPA guide on long-term stewardship, *Built Today, Treasured Tomorrow*, provides further detail, < http://www.tcpa.org.uk/practical-guide-to-long-term-stewardship>, 2014 (accessed 6 September 2016).

2   Further information on this model is available from the websites of the National Community Land Trust Network, <http://www.communitylandtrusts.org.uk>, n.d. and Cooperatives UK, <http://www.uk.coop>, n.d. (both accessed 6 September 2016).

3   See <http://www.communitylandtrusts.org.uk/funding-and-resources/faqs>, n.d. (accessed 6 September 2016).

4   See <http://www.eastlondonclt.co.uk/#/what-is-a-clt/4576878256>, n.d. accessed 6 September 2016).

CHAPTER 11

1   For a detailed description of architecture in the garden cities see: English Heritage, *English Garden Cities: An Introduction*, by Mervyn Miller, 2010.

2   'William Morris, How We Live and How We Might Live' was a lecture delivered to the Hammersmith branch of the Socialist Democratic Federation (SDF) at Kelmscott House on 30 November 1884.

3   Originally German, 'Passivhaus' is an innovative building design standard that, put simply, aims to recycle the heat naturally generated in a building in order to eliminate the need for additional heating. For further details, see <http://www.passivhaus.org.uk/standard.jsp?id=122>, n.d. (accessed 6 September 2016).

4   See <Architecture.com/HomeWise>, n.d. (accessed 6 September 2016).

5   TCPA, New Towns Act 2015? < http://www.tcpa.org.uk/new-towns-act-2015> 2014 (accessed 26 September 2016).

6   TCPA, *New Towns and Garden Cities – Lessons for Tomorrow. Stage 2: Lessons for Delivering a New Generation of Garden Cities*, Published by the Town and Country Planning Association http://www.tcpa.org.uk/lessons-for-tomorrow-stage-2-report, 2015 (accessed 26 September 2016). p15

7   For more details, see <http://www.ashford.gov.uk/chilmington-quality-agreement>, n.d. (accessed 6 September 2016).

CHAPTER 12

1   Simon Evans, 'UN Report: climate pledges fall short of cheapest route to 2C limit', *Carbon Brief*, <http://www.carbonbrief.org/un-report-climate-pledges-fall-short-of-cheapest-route-to-2c-limit>, 2015 (accessed 7 September 2016).

2   For further details, see 'Adapting to climate change', *Committee on Climate Change*, <https://www.theccc.org.uk/tackling-climate-change/preparing-for-climate-change>, n.d. (accessed 7 September 2016).

3   The European Parliament and the Council of the European Union, *Directive 2010/31/EU of the European Parliament and of the Council of 19 May 2010 on the energy performance of buildings*.

4   DCLG, Planning Policy Statement – eco-towns: a supplement to Planning Policy Statement 1, Communities and Local Government Publications, London, 2009, Policy ET 7.

5   For further details on energy masterplanning, see Kate Henderson *Energising Masterplanning*, TCPA report for the EU-SPECIAL Project, Town and Country Planning Association, London, <http://www.special-eu.org/assets/uploads/SPECIAL_EP1.pdf>, 2015 (accessed 7 September 2016).

CHAPTER 13

1   DCLG, *Over a million more people given the chance to own their own home*, press release, Department for Communities and Local Government, London, 26 May 2015, <https://www.gov.uk/government/news/over-a-million-more-people-given-the-chance-to-own-their-own-home>, 2015 (accessed 7 September 2016).

2   Pete Jefferys, *Non-starter homes*, Shelter policy blog, 26 August 2015, <http://blog.shelter.org.uk/2015/08/non-starter-homes>, 2015 (accessed 7 September 2016).

3   DCLG, *National Planning Practice Guidance: Viability and plan making*, <http://planningguidance.communities.gov.uk/blog/guidance/viability-guidance>, 26 March 2015 (accessed 7 September 2016).

4   TCPA, *The future of planning and place making*, Town and Country Planning Association, London, <http://www.tcpa.org.uk/data/files/Future_of_Planning_embargoed_until_19_March_2015.pdf>, 2015 (accessed 7 September 2016).

5   House of Lords Select Committee on National Policy for the Built Environment, *Report of Session 2015–16 Building better places*, TSO, London, <http://www.publications.parliament.uk/pa/ld201516/ldselect/ldbuilt/100/100.pdf>, 2016 (accessed 7 September 2016).

6   DCLG, *Technical housing standards – nationally described space standard*, Department for Communities and Local Government, London, <https://www.gov.uk/government/publications/technical-housing-standards-nationally-described-space-standard>, 2015 (accessed 7 September 2016).

7   Statistics from census data cited within 'The New Towns Record. Planning Exchange', *Idox Information Service*, <http://www.idoxgroup.com/knowledge-services/idox-information-service/the-new-towns-record.html>, n.d. (accessed 25 August 2016).

CHAPTER 14

1   More detail on these benefits can be found in TCPA, *Improving Culture, Arts and Sporting Opportunities through Planning. A Good Practice Guide*. Town and Country Planning Association, London, <https://www.london.gov.uk/sites/default/files/tcpa_culture_guide.pdf>, 2013, p. 6. (accessed 25 August 2016).

2   See, for example, Ward, C. Anarchy In Milton Keynes, date unknown, published by the Anarchists Library <http://theanarchistlibrary.org/library/colin-ward-anarchy-in-milton-keynes.pdf> (accessed 26 September 2016).

3   Find out more at www.phillymagicgardens.org/about-us, 2016 (accessed 8 September 2016).

4   For more information, see www.uandiplc.com/portfolio/the-old-vinyl-factory-hayes, 2016 (accessed 8 September 2016).

5   For more information, see TCPA, Improving Culture.

6   The detail of how this stewardship model developed, how it is funded and its governance mechanisms can be found in TCPA, Built Today, Treasured Tomorrow – A Good Practice Guide to Long-Term Stewardship, Town and Country Planning Association, London, <http://www.tcpa.org.uk/data/files/TCPA_GC_Stewardship_Guide.pdf>, 2014 (accessed 6 September 2016).

7   For more information, see: <http://www.ifmilton-keynes.org/home.html>, n.d. and <http://www.artscouncil.org.uk/funding/funded-projects/case-studies/milton-keynes-2012-summer-culture-brings-arts-culture-and-64m-city>.

INDEX

INDEX

PICTURE CREDITS

A2 Dominion, 149

Anne Thorne Architects 158l

Alex McGregor [CC BY-SA 2.0 (http://creativecommons.org/licenses/by-sa/2.0/)], via Wikimedia Commons, 9

Andrew Curtis/Creative Commons, 47br

BDP/Nick Caville, Creative Commons: https://commons.wikimedia.org/wiki/File:Stunning_architectural_photographs_of_Essex_Business_School_(24285144282).jpg?uselang=en-gb, 108

Bournville Village Trust, 13bl, 122

Boyd and Evans, 48/49

Building BloQs, 163

By mrpbps (New Lanark & River) [CC BY 2.0 (http://creativecommons.org/licenses/by/2.0)], via Wikimedia Commons, 12

By sashafatcat [CC BY 2.0 (http://creativecommons.org/licenses/by/2.0)], via Wikimedia Commons, 165

Cannock Mill Cohousing Colchester Ltd 158tr & br

Caroline Brown, David Lock Associates, 74, 123

Courtesy of BFI Stills, 37

Cramlington Library, Northumberland Council, 59

Creative Commons (https://commons.wikimedia.org/wiki/File:Pitteuchar,_Glenrothes.jpg?uselang=en-gb), (https://creativecommons.org/licenses/by-sa/3.0/deed.en), 42tr

Creative Commons Licence (https://commons.wikimedia.org/wiki/File:Hellerau,_An_der_Winkelwiese_8-12_%2B_Am_Dorffrieden_2.jpg), 23tr

Creative Commons licence: https://commons.wikimedia.org/wiki/File%3ARio_Rancho_Sprawl.jpeg, 30

Crown Copyright. Contains public sector information licensed under the Open Government Licence v2.0., 63

David Barnes Photography, 167r

David F. Bostock, The Radburn Association, 21tr & 42tl

David Lock Associates, 97, 100, 102, 103, 142/143, 173

'Destination Milton Keynes', 43tr

East Hampshire District Council, 66/67

East London Community Land Trust, 121

Ebbsfleet Development Corporation, 111

From: "From New Towns to Green Politics: Campaigning for Town and Country Planning 1946-1990"by Dennis Hardy, Copyright © 2016 Routledge. Reproduced by permission of Taylor & Francis Books UK., 36, 39

Garden City Collection, Letchworth Garden City Heritage Foundation, 14bl, 19, 20, 21b, 29, 32

Hampstead Garden Suburb Trust, 22

Harlow Council - Planning Department, 46tl

Hertfordshire Archives and Local Studies (HALS), 4

Homes & Communities Agency, courtesy of the City Discovery Centre, Milton Keynes, 49br, 52tl

Homes and Communities Agency, 40tl

Homes and Communities Agency/MK City Discovery Centre, 41, 43tl, 45b, 47cr

IBA Hamburg/Aufwind Luftbilder, 107

Incredible Edible Todmorden team - www.incredible-edible-todmorden.co.uk, 168

Jamie Anson, @jammiefreerider & Acts 29 www.acts29.org.uk, 167tl

John Lewis Partnership Heritage Centre, 31

Joseph Rowntree Housing Trust, 131t, 141

Kirsty Dixon, 172

Lancaster co-housing, 131br

Leila Fielding, 164

Letchworth Garden City Heritage Foundation, 106, 118tl, 129tr, 130, 136tr, 139t, 160

North Lanarkshire Council, 46bl

Proctor and Matthews Architects and Tim Crocker photography, 133t

Reporduced by kind permission of North Hertfordshire Museum Service, 18

RIBA Collections, 47t, 52/53

Runcorn Libraries - Halton Borough Council, 44

Shelter / KPMG / Project 00, 71

Shuffle Festival and photographer Elena Heatherwick, 170

Sludge G / Flickr Creative Commons License / https://www.flickr.com/photos/sludgeulper/3525479833/in/photolist-6nx2HP-6nx1k4-6nB9yL-6nx2fX-6nwZMi/), 11

Social Life Social Sustainability framework, taken from "Design for Social Sustainability" (Social Life 2012)., 160

The Art of Building a Home. A collection of lectures and illustartions by Barry parker and Raymond Unwin, 1901 (2nd Ed.), 166

The Labour Party, 34

TCPA, 2, 13br, 16, 21tl, 23b, 26, 27, 29, 35, 38, 40tr, 45t, 60, 61, 64, 66tl, 77, 72, 76bl, 81, 82, 86, 93, 98, 99, 101, 116, 118/119, 129tl, 134, 135, 136tl, 137, 138, 139bl, 140, 144, 147br, 150, 154, 156/157, 159, 162, 170, 174

Tony Ray-Jones / RIBA Collections, 58

Unilever Archives & Records, Unilver Plc, 13t

Wei Yang and Partners, 114/115